HOW TO I
BY T

G000256745

HOW TO
INCREASE SALES
BY TELEPHONE

ALFRED TACK

CEDAR

A Mandarin Paperback

HOW TO INCREASE SALES BY TELEPHONE

First published by Cedar 1978
This edition published 1990 by Cedar
an imprint of Mandarin Paperbacks
Michelin House, 81 Fulham Road, London SW3 6RB

Mandarin is an imprint of the Octopus Publishing Group

Copyright © 1971 by Alfred Tack

A CIP catalogue record for this title
is available from the British Library
ISBN 0 7493 0717 X

Printed in Great Britain
by Cox and Wyman Ltd, Reading

Contents

CHAPTER 1

The Telephone Market

Deciding to buy a new car I telephoned a British company for information.

Their telephone operator told me the line to the salesman was engaged and asked me whether I wanted to hold on or ring back. I held on.

Eventually I spoke to a salesman and asked, 'Can you tell me the overall length and width of Model X?'

This simple question stumped him. He asked me to hold on while he found a brochure. Several minutes later he returned to the telephone and gave me the dimensions, adding, 'Anything else you want to know?'

'No,' I answered.

'O.K. then. Good-bye.'

There was not the slightest effort on his part to gain my interest, neither did he ask my name and address. And car manufacturers are always complaining of the difficulties of marketing during periods of credit restriction.

I wrote to another distributor of a well-known British car. The sales manager posted a catalogue to me in response to my request for details, but he did not enclose a covering letter, only a compliment slip. I heard no more from him.

Is this a diatribe against British manufacturers and distributors? Not at all. The distribution of foreign cars proved to be just as bad. The sales manager in charge of the distribution of an American car wrote a good letter which included the sentences:

A demonstration model is available, and I shall gladly arrange a test drive to suit your convenience. Should you require any further information please don't hesitate to contact me.

I did not contact him—and he didn't contact me.

The letter from the distributor of a German car was signed by a secretary per pro the sales manager. Here is an extract:

. . . If, after studying the literature, you feel that you would like a demonstration please don't hesitate to contact the writer, who will be pleased to make the necessary arrangements.

Here we have examples of inefficient salesmanship. It is a salesman's job to try to convert every prospect into a buyer, and he should telephone every prospective buyer within twenty-four hours of receiving an enquiry.

Why don't they do so? The answer is that telephone selling is still in its infancy. Some fear to use the telephone, others treat it too casually. Many take the coward's way out and prefer to write letters rather than face up to a person to person call.

Avis achieved success in the car hire world by claiming that as No. 2 to Hertz they had to try harder. They certainly did as far as telephone usage was concerned. The president of Avis had a separate telephone line specially installed in his office. He advertised the fact, and invited anyone with a complaint to telephone him direct. He didn't receive many calls, but his enlightened action brought the company a lot of publicity.

How different from the attitude of one of our leading appliance manufacturers.

The wife of a friend purchased a dish-washer which did a first-class job. Having great difficulty in obtaining a small easily fitted replacement part from the supplier, her husband wrote a personal letter to the service manager of the appliance manufacturer. Although it was a letter of complaint, he went out of his way to mention that his firm used many different pieces of equipment manufactured by the appliance company, and had always been satisfied with their machines and service.

Ten days later he received a compliment slip from the customer-relations department of the company advising him that a replacement had been sent.

Why couldn't the service manager have replied personally to my friend's letter? Or better still, telephoned to show his concern at what had happened. He could then have apologised for not writing a letter and explained that the first priority was for the replacement part to be sent. He could have thanked my friend for the kind way in which he had written.

If he had taken this action my friend would quickly have forgotten the bad service, but would have remembered for a long time the efficiency and courtesy of the service manager.

There are so many similar opportunites to increase sales and goodwill by better use of the telephone.

The Follow Up

It would seem obvious that enquiries, requests for brochures, and response to advertising should be followed up quickly, yet this only happens in the most efficient companies. Often, the standard practice is either to post the brochure or to send the enquiry on to a salesman to deal with. If an advertising campaign pulls well, salesmen can have more enquiries than they can handle quickly. The result is a delayed call and, perhaps, an order lost.

If there is the possibility of the salesman's call being delayed then it is more efficient to use the telephone as a follow-up. The advantage of this is twofold. The prospect's interest is maintained, and the telephone salesman can evaluate the strength of the enquiry. It may be that it is so weak that it would not pay a salesman to call at all; there are always a number of enquiries received from direct mail advertising shots and advertising campaigns which are of no value.

The telephone may be used:

(a) to make a sale;
(b) to make an appointment for a salesman to call;
(c) to service the prospect until a salesman can call;
(d) to check whether a brochure has arrived, or to evaluate the strength of the enquiry.

A tailor in a small way of business advertised regularly his made-to-measure sports jackets and trousers in a newspaper's *Saturday Postal Bargain* columns. On receipt of an enquiry he would send patterns, and hope for an order. The response was poor, so he changed his policy. Five days after the patterns had been sent he telephoned the prospect (directory enquiries were kept busy, so he said) and explained fully the specialised service he was offering. The result was 80% conversion of enquiries into sales, against

25% previously. He now has a flourishing mail order business in men's wear.

A garage proprietor instituted a sales drive for tyres. Six months after a car was sold, either new or second-hand, his salesmen would telephone the customer to check on the tyre wear. If the customer told him that there was still good tread on the tyres he would check again three months later. Sales of tyres increased by 30%.

A wine merchant regularly telephones his customers advising them of special shipments of wine. The customers feel flattered, often purchase the wines, and also order other drinks at the same time.

Every marketing organisation should consider what additional business can be obtained by using the telephone for following up enquiries or selling extras to customers.

Keeping Out Competition
The marketing policy of a company supplying office equipment is dynamic. They train their salesmen well, and all enquiries are followed up within twenty-four hours. One of their best accounts is an insurance company, looked after by a senior salesman.

After booking a repeat order for twenty-four new typewriters he believed that he had satisfied their needs for several months ahead. Five weeks after the new typewriters had been delivered the accounts department needed a special long carriage machine.

A competitor had been calling on the insurance company every month in the hope of getting some business from them. He called once more on the day the request was made for the long carriage machine.

He got the order, became very friendly with the buyer, obtained more business later, and then became firmly entrenched.

Too many marketing directors and salesmen believe that no one can take business away from accounts which they have had for years. They forget the age-old dictum,

Never forget a customer–never let a customer forget you.

The best way of maintaining contact and keeping competition at bay is to service customers regularly by telephone in between the salesman's calls.

If this had been the policy of the company selling typewriters, apparently so efficiently, they would have maintained their monopoly instead of having to share the business with a competitor.

In the consumer field it is standard practice to telephone retailers for repeat business. It should also be a marketing tool for those companies on consumer durables and the capital equipment field.

The wise sales manager inaugurates a system of regular following up by telephone on all large quotations, knowing that competitors' quotations are also being considered.

Making Appointments

This is a five-star aid to salesmanship, and it is surprising that it is so neglected. Often a salesman is left to make his own appointments in his own way, which may be the wrong way, because he is not trained in telephone techniques. More and more companies are, however, engaging telephone sales girls to make appointments for their sales staff. It cannot be right for a highly paid salesman to spend perhaps a full day a week making appointments for the following four days. Far better to employ telephone sales girls to make these appointments for the sales force. Each girl should be able to keep three salesmen fully booked up with appointments.

When a company selling accounting machinery adopted this procedure sales increased by 20%–but then, the salesmen were making 20% more contacts.

Evaluating Applicants

The standard procedure for engaging salesmen is to advertise the vacancy, consider letters sent in by applicants, select those whose qualifications line up with the job specification, and send them application forms. When these forms are returned and evaluated, selected salesmen are invited to attend an interview.

The expense of bringing salesmen long distances (it doesn't pay a sales manager to travel many miles to interview one man) is considerable, and it can be time wasting. Under these circumstances, an initial telephone call can:

   enable the sales manager to evaluate further the applicant's potential;
   enable the applicants to decide whether or not it is the type of job they want;
   save a wasted and expensive journey.

To Increase Goodwill

When there is a delivery problem, why wait until a complaint is received? Far better to telephone the customer and explain the reason for the delay.

A 'thank you' for a worthwhile order is always well received by a customer, because this courtesy is so unusual.

Rather than send out a printed invitation to view a new range of goods, telephone and make the invitation really personal.

If merchandise has to be substituted it is better to telephone than to write a stereotyped note explaining the reason for this substitution.

The telephone can be used to give good news quickly to customers, or to explain why lines are out of stock.

Finding Dealers

Dealerships can be set up more quickly by using the telephone than by writing a letter to make the initial contact. A would-be dealer always appreciates a call from a top executive, and the franchise can often be closed on the 'phone. If not, the salesman will find it much easier to finalise the arrangements when he calls.

To Obtain Leads

Use your users is one of the oldest tags in selling. It still remains true. Your users are your best friends, and are often willing to supply leads if asked for them. When you service a customer by telephone, to make sure that he is satisfied with his purchase add,

'Mr. Jones, I am sure you have a friend or business acquaintance who would also want . . .'

Wholesalers

The death-knell of wholesalers has been sounded many times, but the efficient wholesaler can play a most important part in the marketing plan. Some wholesalers only wait for business to arrive, while others employ *order takers* who have little time to spare for selling.

The main service offered by a wholesaler is a quick replacement of stock. Efficient use of the telephone is essential for wholesale marketing. A trained operator can save the salesman's time, allowing him to sell more profitable lines and increase turnover.

Selling Direct
The direct telephone selling market is growing fast. Telephone sales girls sell magazine subscriptions, advertising, consumer goods, cosmetics, while telephone salesmen sell insurance (increases), cleaning services, decorating, consumer durables.

Save Writing a Letter
It's cheaper and quicker to telephone.

Customer Reaction To New Products
Market research can be carried out more rapidly over the telephone.

Maintaining Contact With Service Engineers
Service engineers are notoriously bad users of time. Telephone checks are better than reports received three days after the event.

Credit Restrictions
When goods are held up because credit has been exceeded, a telephone call can do two things:

(a) get the account paid;
(b) get the goods flowing to the customer again.

To write a letter under these circumstances may result in the customer ignoring the letter and going to a competitor for similar goods.

To Rescind Cancellations

Salesmen often find it hard to reinstate orders. Sometimes they avoid making calls on dissatisfied customers, but a head office executive telephoning can often win back the customer.

Check on Advertising

Don't leave it to the advertising agent to tell you that the advertisement is brilliant. Check up yourself to make certain that the advertisement is appreciated by customers, dealers, and salesmen.

Enquiries

Get them to the salesmen quickly, by telephone. While a postman is sorting out the letters, another company could be booking the order.

Small Accounts

It often doesn't pay to send a salesman to small traders. It does pay to keep those traders on the books by telephone selling.

Uncovered Territory

Cold canvass telephone calls on prospects trading in open territories can lead to a build up of accounts which may warrant the allocation of the territory to a salesman at a later date.

Selling the Extra

It sometimes isn't possible for a salesman to sell all the *extras* at an initial sale. One of the companies in our group, Nu-aire Ltd., obtains 15% of service contracts over the telephone.

Collecting Overdue Accounts

Credit control should be included in the overall marketing plan so that the cash flow can be maintained. Without a good cash flow sales programmes may have to be cut. Collecting accounts by telephone is, therefore, a selling job.

Special Opportunities

The Board Appointments and Changes columns in the national dailies can be used to find leads. Executives who have been promoted to senior positions may require a new car, or they may be thinking about moving to a larger house or installing a swimming pool.

Seasons

The salesman selling unit heating appliances can contact many more prospects by telephone during the months of September than he can ever do by personal calling.

The salesman selling garden furniture can carry out similar cold canvass telephoning in early summer.

Weddings and Engagements

Newlyweds, or those about to be married, are always good prospects for furniture, houses, jewellery, clothing and travel.

New Factory Premises

Get in first by telephoning when a factory is being designed or built. It enables the salesman to find and make the right contacts.

It is no use being second when selling vending

machines, canned music, frozen food cabinets for canteens, office furniture and typewriters.

There are many opportunities for increasing business by telephone selling, the market is wide open, waiting to be tapped.

CHAPTER 2

Everyone Sells

Scene: A general office

'Hello.'

'Can I speak to Mr. Brown please?'

'Who is speaking?'

'I want to talk to Mr. Brown.'

'But I must know who's calling.'

'Smith, of Smith's Pumps.'

'What is it about?'

'I have a price query.'

'Then you want the order department.'

'No, I want to speak to Mr. Brown.'

'Well he isn't in *yet*.'

'When will he be in?'

'About half an hour's time, I should think . . .'

And that shorthand-typist, masquerading under the title of secretary, doesn't believe she has a selling function.

Scene: A managing director's office

'Johnson here.'

'Good morning Mr. Johnson, it's White again, of White's Ltd. You will remember I spoke to you last week about the delivery of the steel partitioning. It still hasn't arrived.'

'Mr. White, I told you that we are, unfortunately, a little behind with deliveries and that you should take the matter up with our Mr. Tilling.'

'I can't get any satisfaction from Mr. Tilling, that's why I am telephoning you.'

'It's not my line of country. You can't expect me to go chasing every order we get, can you?'

'No, but we're in real trouble, and your salesman knew the position when I placed the order. We must have the partitioning fixed before most of the staff return from their holidays.'

'I'm sorry, we've all got our troubles. You really must deal with Mr. Tilling.'

'But I just told you –'

'Good God man, what do you expect me to do, bring the bloody stuff myself? . . . '

That managing director doesn't think he is concerned in any way with selling. He prides himself on being a highly efficient administrator.

Scene: A credit control department

'Mr. Green, unless we have your cheque by Friday we will take proceedings.'

'What the hell do you mean? Your salesman pestered me for months to open the account and said that two months' credit was normal.'

'It was, once. It isn't now. There's a squeeze on. I've written you three letters.'

'Your salesman said it was routine –'

'I'm not concerned with what the salesman said. My job is to collect, and I must have your cheque by Friday.'

And that credit control manager doesn't believe that he has a selling job to do.

Scene: A service department

'My washing machine has broken down again. Can you send a mechanic quickly?'

'Just a minute.'

'It's very urgent.'

'Everything's urgent. Hold on. . . . O.K. Mrs. Harris, I'll send someone next Friday-week.'

'But that's in ten days' time.'

'And that's doing you a favour. I have three men away ill, and we're short of staff, anyway.'

'But I have five children. . . .'

'That's not my fault, Mrs. Harris. Ten days is the very best I can do.'

And that service manager doesn't believe he is any way involved in selling.

All these examples are true, only the names have been changed. They were sent to me in response to my request for examples of bad treatment over the telephone.

I sent out fifty letters and thirty examples of inefficiency in telephone communication were returned to me. Nine other correspondents wrote to say that they had never had cause for complaint, and eleven did not reply.

Why is it that normally friendly and courteous people change when they use a telephone? Why is this allowed to happen in business?

Everyone in an organisation is a part of a marketing plan, and included in that plan must be telephone selling. One person can undo all the brilliant work of a salesman in opening an account, or can hinder his negotiations for a large order.

One of our consultants working on an assignment was discussing with the buyer of packaging material the products and services offered by various suppliers. During the conversation he asked the reason for the sharp drop in purchases from a well-known public company.

The buyer, a woman, answered, 'I hate telephoning *them*. No one ever seems interested, *they* always have that couldn't-care-less attitude.'

The significant words are *them* and *they*. What the buyer should have said was, *she* or *him*.

Because an individual had failed to appreciate his or her specific communication responsibilities the whole organisation was condemned.

In the same way as all male car drivers believe that they are highly skilled, and most women consider themselves to be fashion conscious, so the majority of people mislead themselves into believing that they know how to communicate efficiently by telephone. In consequence of this mistaken belief, some business men are abrupt, considering that others waste time on the telephone. The psychological reason for their abruptness is often that the telephone gives them an opportunity of being masterful without having to look someone straight in the eye. Others are garrulous and can never conclude a conversation except after several good-byes. They believe they are showing courtesy and friendship, when they are only proving their lack of knowledge of telephone techniques.

Then there are the men and women who mumble, or whose voices are indistinct because they hold the mouthpiece at arms length as if it were ridden with deadly bacteria.

The art of telephone communication in industry must be learned. Experience since childhood does not guarantee *telefficiency*. Experience may only result in the perpetuation of mistakes. Telephone communication does *not* come naturally to people. Joe Louis, heavyweight champion of the world from 1937–1948, and one of the all-time greats in boxing once said, 'People read that I was born with the movements of a panther. The truth is that I was a very clumsy kid. The footwork they called "catsense" was something Chappie Blackburn drilled into me. That was learnt, it wasn't a "born" thing.'

Check

You can prove something for yourself right now, if the time is between 9 a.m. and 5 p.m.

Pick up your telephone and ring consecutively five different companies advertising their products or services in a newspaper or magazine, and including a telephone number in their advertisement. Ask for further details of the goods or services they are offering. Totally, you will speak probably to fifteen different people at least – five telephone operators and five go-betweens who will then pass you on to five others who may come up with the right information. Try it. You won't prove me wrong. Yet these *telesellers* believe themselves to be expert handlers of the telephone.

If anything, in this example, the number of people you will speak to is an underestimation. You will be fortunate if you are not passed on two or three times. You will receive a 'hallo' greeting from most of the staff, which doesn't help the conversation along at all. You will hold on for considerable periods, because you have been requested to hold on, and in the end you will wonder whether or not the operator has passed away.

If you telephone a retail store you will either not get through to the department at all, or when you do get through to the department you will have to beg someone to sell you something.

You will agree, after making this test, that there is a lot of profit to be made out of the intelligent use of the telephone. That a case has been made out for the training of all staff who handle the telephone – but wait a moment! How about us? Do we sometimes fall by the wayside? Are we ever self-critical?

We must always remember that everyone in industry who speaks on the telephone, sells.

The techniques taught in this book, learned from a lifetime of selling, therefore apply to everyone in industry, but most of all to those who live by being effective communicators – the salesmen.

CHAPTER 3

The Telephone Sales Presentation

Have you ever had to ask your bank manager for a large overdraft? You have. Then you will remember how carefully you laid your plans, and how you rehearsed your appeal over and over again.

Remember the way you decided to build his confidence in you by quickly telling him of your promotion? Do you recollect the way you explained the many assets of the house you wanted to buy? Highly praised by the surveyor, a bargain compared to others in the vicinity, what a wonderful state of repair it was in, how it would save you money on fares to the office, its beautiful surroundings. . . .

Whether you believe it or not that was selling and, in fact, you were making a well-thought-out sales presentation because you didn't want to leave anything to chance.

Have you ever had to make an important speech? You have. Remember the elation you felt on receiving the request, followed by the despair as you contemplated the enormity of the task?

But you thought and thought around the subject. Then you wrote out the speech in full, didn't you? Tried to remember it, and failed. Then you edited the speech, got the gist of it, and found that brief notes helped you to remember the flow of scintillating, humorous, gripping, vital sentences. But you rehearsed right up to the day of the speech. You mouthed the words on your way to work, and you mouthed them again on the way home.

That is exactly what most sensible people do when preparing a speech, and most sensible salesmen do when preparing a mini-speech to sell on the telephone.

Yet some salesmen believe that they have no need for a prepared presentation, although those same men who believe they can sell off the cuff, even rehearse the excuses they are going to make to their wives when they stay out late.

At our sales training courses a full session is devoted to the phenomenon of men and women who daily use a sales sequence in their private lives, but do not believe it is necessary to master a sales presentation for sales interviews.

The logic behind the sales sequence is unanswerable. If there is one best way to present a case why use a string of words which add up to second best?

It has sometimes been said that selling begins when the buyer says 'No'. This, of course, is now known to be nonsense. The art of salesmanship is to employ words so skilfully that the big 'No' in the buyer's mind at the commencement of the sale diminishes into the little 'no' of an answerable objection, and then disappears altogether.

The weak salesman – or even the strong salesman with the poor sales sequence – often does not get past the first 'NO'. If he does, he has to fight a very hard battle to retrieve his cause.

The good sales presentation, therefore, can be the greatest of all problem solvers for the telephone salesman, because it will hold a buyer's interest and answer many of his objections without him having to voice them.

IT'S TOUGH

It is harder to sell a six-inch double column of space in a magazine by telephone than it would be if face to face with the buyer. It is more difficult to persuade a prospect to buy insurance over the telephone than when your eyes are looking into his at an interview. It is tougher to sell a new range of products to a grocer over the telephone than it would be for the salesman making one of his regular visits. That is why the telephone salesman must have a really tough streak if he is to stay with his job. Like a cold canvassing salesman who works shop after shop or house after house, he has to take so many *noes* to obtain that *yes*. There is nothing unusual in this to a speciality salesman, but other salesmen using the telephone to increase sales have to learn it the hard way. The well thought out sales sequence will increase the *yesses*, and decrease the *noes*.

Telephone selling is also tough because all of the appeal is through the ear. The majority of people are bad listeners, and buyers who are not eager to make a purchase, or prospects interrupted by the call during their routine work have *cottonwool eardrums*. They do not concentrate on what is being explained to them, and the salesman cannot command their immediate interest by the use of visual aids. The buyer cannot see the brightness of the salesman's eyes, the enthusiasm of his bearing or be influenced by his winning personality. Neither can the telephone salesman involve the buyer's senses of smell, touch, taste or sight.

He is not able to say, 'Isn't this perfume an aromatic heaven?' or 'Just feel the smoothness of the cloth,' or

'This taste is unique, isn't it?' or 'Look at the photograph of this burned factory.'

The challenge to the telephone salesman is to overcome these obstacles inherent in this form of communication and build a sales presentation which will command a hearing. It must be designed to make the buyer agree, approve, and act.

GOLDEN WORDS

During the first session on the second day of our telephone sales training course the instructor begins by saying, 'You live by the words you use. . . .'

Salesmen selling person to person are assisted by brochures, drawings, letters, samples, or demonstration models, but the telephone salesman depends solely on the *words he uses*. He must, therefore, polish every word, every sentence until he is positive that they have the right balance to tip the scales in his favour.

He must not use indecisive words such as:

possibly
maybe
I think
could be

He must try to use one word instead of two or more. Instead of: Use:

Instead of:	Use:
in as much as	*since*
with a view to	*to*
for that reason	*so*
on a basis of	*by*
according to our records	*we find*

check our records	check
a large number of	many
along the lines of	like
during the time that	while
in consideration of	considering
in view of the fact that	because
in the very near future	soon
without making any noise	noiselessly

Also, more expressive, descriptive words should be used:

Instead of:	Use:
it is a fine design	it is an exquisite design
you will get good results	you will get excellent results
it has a bright finish	it has a glowing finish
it will remove odours	it will banish odours
we are sorry you are dissatisfied	your frank comments are appreciated

The telephone salesman can only use a few hundred words to complete a sales story. Face to face he could be using two to four thousand words. Another reason for every word having punch, power, and appeal.

PRE-PLANNING

Analysis by self questioning is essential if the presentation is to have depth and appeal.

QUESTION 1

Have I complete product knowledge?
Can your company deliver from stock? If not, what is

the time lag? Are all colours in stock? Can specials be supplied? What are the technical advantages of your product? What is the technical advantage claimed by your competitors? What service do you offer? Does your company service equipment through dealers or direct? What is the service time lag? Is there a charge for installation? Are you conversant with all forms of packaging? What credit terms are offered? Are you up to date with all advertising plans, sales promotion schemes, merchandising? Do you understand the small print on the agreements or policies? . . .

QUESTION 2
What is the general market for my products?
This can readily be answered in the consumer field (not forgetting canteens, hospitals, clubs, etc.) but if you are selling capital equipment or a specialised service, then more research may be necessary. For example:

Selling advertising space
Space salesmen sell in the main through advertising agents, but there are other fields worth investigating. Space could be sold direct to the smaller manufacturer or retailer or dealer who may not have an agent, while selling classified advertising direct to the public is still hardly touched upon.

Selling insurance
Everyone needs insurance, and most of the likely prospects are contacted regularly by insurance salesmen. Very few insurance salesmen call on retail shops, however. Would that be a market?

Publicans are better listeners to salesmen than managing directors yet they, again, are rarely contacted by insurance salesmen unless they have made an enquiry. Also, publicans can give leads for further business.

What other outlets are there?

Selling office equipment

The larger offices and factories have obviously the greatest buying potential, but there are other outlets which the telephone salesman could investigate. Restaurant proprietors buy typewriters, but are seldom sold them. Small hotel owners are rarely contacted. Ex-secretaries who offer a typing service can also be contacted. They should change their typewriters regularly.

These examples could be multiplied many times and applied to every industry. Extra outlets can be discovered and covered quickly by the telephone salesman.

QUESTION 3
Why should anyone buy my products?

The kernel of the sales presentation must stress the benefits to the buyer. The salesman can only unearth these benefits if he is aware of the main reasons why his prospect or customer needs his service or products.

Turning needs into wants

Many a prospect may need your product, but he may not want it, and the majority of buyers satisfy their *wants* rather than their *needs*.

He may *need* insurance, but *want* an extra holiday. The house may *need* rewiring, but she *wants* a fur coat.

He may *need* a computer, but he *wants* a new head office built in country surroundings.

He *needs* extra stock, but he *wants* cash in the bank.

He *needs* a series of advertisements, but he *wants* to economise.

What will be the decision of those buyers if their mind is not influenced by a salesman? They will decide on their *wants*.

The insurance salesman must convince his prospect that for the sake of his family he should forgo that extra holiday and give his wife and children immediate protection in the event of his death.

The electrical contractor will point out to the householder the great risk she is running of fire, so that she will *want* to have her house rewired before buying the fur coat.

The managing director must be persuaded that there would be little sense in a head office in the country if his business efficiency suffered. The salesman must convince the managing director to *want* the computer more than the country surroundings.

The salesman selling consumer durables must stress to the buyer the risk he is running in losing business to his competitors when he runs down stock, and that the stocks will bring him a greater return than will be received from bank deposits.

The advertiser must be made to realise that to insert only one advertisement is false economy.

The sales presentation must be so strong that the *need* for product or service will be turned into the greatest possible *want*, and so overcome the urge of a buyer to spend money in other directions.

STEPS TO THE ORDER

There must be a logical sequence to every sales presentation. The first recorded sales story (the euphemism 'sales presentation' came later) was written by a salesman employed by the National Cash Register Company. Later it became the basis of the sequence used by all NCR salesmen. The AIDA formula became a by-word in selling, and since then, hardly a book on salesmanship has failed to mention AIDA, a sales presentation based on these steps.

A ttention
I nterest
D esire
A ction

This sequence was right, but the very wordy sales story built around it failed because it was meant to be learned verbatim and spoken parrotwise, and men are not parrots.

During the early '30's we changed the AIDA formula to embrace additional steps, but made it easier to learn because the salesman had only to memorise a few sentences. The salesman, or sales trainer, would write the sequence in full, underlining the lead sentences to each step. Only these lead sentences had to be remembered, because they held the key to the step to the order which followed. That step could be elaborated by the salesman by words of his own choosing. The sentences act as reminders to a salesman to keep to a sequence, but in his own words.

This combined the best of both worlds – the ability to use a complete presentation while, at the same time, expressing one's own personality. Since then, many thousands of salesmen have used the *Tack Selling Sentence* technique successfully. It is just as simple to use with the shortened telephone selling sequence.

The sequence for person to person selling is now:

The Approach
Creation of Interest
Creation of Confidence
The Product Benefits
Creation of Desire
The Close

Main selling and reminder sentences are used for each step, but when covering Product Benefits, four or eight main sentences are used; Product Benefits being the focal point of the presentation.

Every single benefit has to be stressed. A salesman must, therefore, find every reason why the prospect should buy, and these reasons are expressed as *Benefits*.

The Telephone Sequence
The telephone salesman will adopt a procedure similar to that of the person to person salesman but with a difference. Although he will still write the presentation in full, he will only look for one main benefit, and one subsidiary benefit. There is no time in telephone selling to build benefit on benefit.

A telephone salesman selling a range of goods, beauty products, for example, will book orders for the majority of his standard creams and lotions, but build his presentation on the one line that is being specially promoted. The benefits of this special product will be stressed – *the uniquely designed bottle, the new ingredient, the advertising campaign,* etc.

There are other changes in the sequence that the telephone salesman must make. *Creating Interest* can no longer be a separate step, and neither can *Confidence Building. The Approach* must create immediate interest, while confidence building can be used at the most appropriate time during the presentation.

To a salesman who is extremely well known to his customer, confidence building need only be a reminder of the wide publicity the new product is receiving, or the way the old product has steadily increased sales because of the sales promotional plans. If a salesman is unknown to the prospect, then he will have to introduce confidence building a little earlier – 'You have probably heard of us, our Company were the originators of . . .' or '. . . have just linked up with . . . .'

The telephone salesman's logical sequence, therefore, will be:

Approach and Interest
Main Benefit
Subsidiary Benefit   }   Create Confidence
Close

Although, in this chapter, the direct sales presentation is being covered, now is the time to explain that when seeking an interview a sequence has again to be changed.

The sequence for obtaining an interview is:

The Approach
Main Benefit
Benefit of Personal Interview
Appointment Close

Whether you are selling a range of goods or capital equipment, whether you sell insurance or advertising signs, whether you sell space or whether you only use the telephone to obtain appointments, always remember that the pre-planning of a sales presentation is the sure way to success.

THE APPROACH

Put yourself in the shoes of your buyer or prospect, for example the owner of a grocery shop, an office manager or a managing director. Men with no time to spare during the day, but having priorities to enable them to use their time effectively.

The salesman calling upon a grocer busily serving a customer, stands aside and waits until the grocer finishes the transaction. That grocer, however, is determined to check his stock as soon as his customer leaves. The arrival of the salesman faces him with two alternatives: He can dismiss the salesman with a 'Sorry, I'm busy', or he can see the salesman and put off stocktaking.

How the salesman acts during the first few seconds after the grocer's customer has left the shop will determine whether or not he is allowed to stay and sell.

The office manager spends his time dictating, attending meetings, interviewing applicants for positions, completing forms. . . . He, therefore, will also have little free time except during meal breaks.

The managing director, if he is efficient, will have a timetable worked out for him by his secretary to which he will adhere – a time for meetings, a time for problem solving, a time for visiting factories. . . .

So now you have a picture of three busy men – a grocer, an office manager, and a managing director – into whose shoes you are going to step.

How would you react if your task of the moment was interrupted by an unexpected telephone call?

If you were the grocer how would feel when the customer is leaving, the salesman is trying to persuade you to see him, the stock needs checking, and the telephone bell rings and a supplier wants to talk about a new promotional effort?

You are now the office manager. The managing director has just been tearing strips off you for staff slackness in the office, and as he is about to leave the telephone bell rings and someone wants to sell you a typewriter.

Now, as a managing director you are worrying about the cash flow, concerned at falling sales, dictating letters and memoranda to the accountant and the sales manager. The telephone bell rings – it is a salesman wanting to increase your insurances.

All executives, shop owners, doctors, or dentists are faced with this problem of how to allocate their time, and they never allow for the unexpected telephone call. No director will tell his secretary to leave free a few minutes in every hour to accept telephone calls from strangers, or comparative strangers.

Whatever time of the day you telephone, your customer or prospect will be busy. A doctor will be about to see a patient, a dentist perhaps talking to his mechanic, a space buyer involved in data analysis. . . . It is only by evolving an interesting and compelling approach that you will make a prospect or buyer put aside what he is doing and listen.

There is a choice of many alternatives when considering the approach you will use. It could be based on one of the following:

a fact
a question
something topical
something to arouse curiosity
a reference from a friend or business associate
advertising
a TV campaign
an exhibition
a letter written previously
a gift
fear
a service
a promotional campaign
a bargain offer

Here are some examples of various approaches:

QUESTION APPROACH

'Mr. John Brown?'
'Yes.'

Repeat name

'Mr. Brown, this is Tom Smith of the Decorative Flower Company. Do you find that a high proportion of women make the bookings for family holidays?'
'Yes, that's true.'
'Mr. Brown, then a bowl of our gorgeous artificial flowers placed in your window would attract attention. They are real window stoppers. . . ,'

REFERENCE APPROACH	'Mr. Arthur White?' 'Yes.'
Repeat name, and make courtesy request	'Mr. White, can you spare me a few moments?' 'Yes.' 'This is Tom Smith of Direct Supplies Ltd. Recently we were able to make drastic reductions in the cost of carbon paper for your friend Mr. Lever of Lever & Jenkins. He told me he felt sure you would want to make similar savings and suggested that I telephone you. . . .'
FEAR APPROACH	'Mr. Green?' 'Yes.'
Repeat name	'Mr. Green, this is Tom Smith of Causeway Garages. It's just ten months since you purchased your car from us. When you called in for petrol the other day our attendant noticed that the treads on your tyres were wearing. You know, Mr. Green, sometimes we only discover a tyre problem when it's too late. . . .'
BARGAIN APPROACH	'Mr. Blue?' 'Yes.'
Repeat name	'Mr. Blue, this is Tom Smith of Apex Toiletries. My reason for

calling you is that new price schedules are coming into effect on the first. As an old and loyal customer I wanted to give you the special opportunity of placing an order now for your forward requirements . . . .'

Study the list of suggested approaches and attempt to ally each one of them to your product or service. This will prove the practicability of evolving novel but strong approaches.

After carrying out the exercise you will decide on the main appeal of your product or service. You will change the approach, at intervals, because selling is not static. Your company may launch a new advertising campaign or a new product. Trial and error may prove to you that the factual approach is better than an advertising approach. You will, however, always keep to an approach that immediately arouses interest, irrespective of how tired you may become of using it. If it works, it's right.

THE MAIN AND SUBSIDIARY BENEFITS

If you are selling a house, does your client buy it from you because of the depth of its foundation, specially glazed bricks facing the outside walls, solidity of structure? Or does he buy because of the pride he will feel in his new home, future capital appreciation, the warmth of the central heating, and the easy-work kitchen?

If you are selling a new line in packet soups, does the caterer buy from you because of the freshness of the vegetables used, or the modern conversion plant or new airtight packaging, or because he believes that the new packet soups will please his customers and increase his margin of profit?

Why do People Buy?

People buy for personal benefit, to satisfy a human need. The main consideration of a space buyer contemplating advertising in a magazine is: will it bring in enough enquiries to make the advertisement profitable? A secondary benefit might be pride in the impact the advertisement will make on his customers. A third benefit, the praise he may receive from his managing director for the success of the campaign.

If a telephone salesman selling space were trying to close the order with that buyer he would, therefore, make his main benefit *profit*, and his secondary benefit *satisfaction* of pride or *to gain praise*.

Parents buy for the good health or amusement of children, managing directors sometimes buy to increase their own ego.

Company reports published in newspapers are often not intended to inform so much as to raise the status of the chairman or managing director in the eyes of *the city*. A retailer could buy because of his fear – fear that if he did not become a *blue and white stamp* trader a competitor might get in first and take away some of his business.

In the industrial world, the main buying reason is nearly always gain of money or the saving of money, but there is a wide variety of subsidiary reasons, and in telephone selling we can only give the *main* benefit and one *subsidiary* benefit.

The following buying motivators are not all embracing, but they will cover 80–90% of buying reasons:

gain of money
saving money
satisfaction of caution
satisfaction of pride
to avoid effort
comfort
sentiment
pleasure
health
to satisfy hunger
utility value
envy
love
to obtain security
to obtain more leisure
to satisfy ego
to protect family
to attract opposite sex
to gain popularity
to gain praise
safety
to possess beautiful objects
to impress others.

Product Analysis

The next step in building the sales presentation is company and product analysis.

Sometimes it is essential to prove a need first, but always a need must be turned into a want.

Before this objective can be reached we must define the main reasons for the prospect or customer wanting a product or service.

This want will stem from the benefits which he will derive from the product, reinforced by the confidence he has in the company and its ability to maintain quality, promises of delivery etc.

First, then, must come company analysis.

Is the company the leader in its field?

When was it established?

What are its future plans?

Where are its factories? (Parochialism still exists.)

How many personnel are engaged in research?

Who is head of the research division? What is his background?

Is the managing director known in any sphere other than his own?

Next must come product analysis.

Is it new?

How long has it been on the market?

Is it derived from a successful predecessor?

Why is it ahead of competitor's products?

How is it constructed?

Why is it less expensive?

Why is it more expensive?

Has it prestige value?

Is it better packed?

Is it covered by a long term guarantee?

Is the brand widely known?

Does it hold the greater share of the market?

Is demand increasing?

Can quick service be carried out?

Can it be adapted specially for a customer?

Is it a novelty?

Will it sell all the year round?

The product analysis must be in depth, and only when all the benefits are listed can the telephone salesman begin to work out his own presentation. This is how one salesman set about the task.

Case Study

A telephone salesman selling an extractor/ventilator fan to an office manager needing a unit for his typing pool, lists product facts, benefits, and buying reasons:

Silent in operation.	Because noise affects health– *health benefits*.
Stops condensation	Decoration needed at less frequent intervals – *saves money*.
Slimline outline.	As unit is visible outside the building – *satisfies pride*.
Unit extracts at 41,000 cfh.	Better atmosphere will result in increased output of staff – *profit*.
Draught free.	Desks can be placed near windows. Better use of office space – *saves money*.
Unit ventilates at 43,000 cfh.	Less risk of infection – *fear*. Less absenteeism – *saves money*.
Extracts smoke.	Smoke discolours decorations and impregnates furnishings – *saves money*.
Extracts odours.	Working in odour-free atmosphere – *gives pleasure*.

Gives exact air changes required.	*Utility value.*
Metal non-corrosive.	Long life, easy maintenance – *saves money*.
Protective grilles.	Less risk of accident – *security*.
Three year guarantee.	*Satisfaction of caution.*

This analysis shows there are five buying reasons for *saving money* and one each for *profit*, *pride*, *fear*, *pleasure*, *caution*, *utility value*, *security*, *health*.

Although, in this example, there are five *saving money* buying reasons, this does not necessarily mean that when analysing products the main benefit must always be based on the majority of buying reasons shown by analysis: but in this case study the salesman decides to concentrate on *saving money* as the main benefit which must lead to increased profitability.

Which means that
The salesman knows that his prospects are not really interested in technicalities, but only the benefits they derive from them. He therefore reminds himself that he must always express benefits in terms of buyers' interests. In order never to forget this fact during a presentation he uses three link words:

which means that
This is how he would use the link words:
'It is silent in operation Mr. Brown *which means that* the health of your staff will not be affected by noise.'

'It stops condensation, Mr. Smith, *which means that* you will save money by decorating less frequently.'

'Mr. White, the metal is non-corrosive, *which means*

that the Nu-aire will have a long life, the maintenance is easy and it will always keep its new look.'

Always remember the words *which means that*.

The salesman now concentrates on building the lead in sentences:

main and subsidiary benefits.

Having made the decision to concentrate on saving money and increasing profits he looks again at the twelve features of his unit and concludes that he will have to stress the benefits of working in a clean fresh atmosphere. Finally he compiles the sentence:

You can turn an eight hour day into an eight hour working day.

That is the sentence he will memorise and on which he will build his step, by noting points to remember:

*staff work better in a clean atmosphere

*no falling off of work in afternoon due to fuggy atmosphere.

Next he concentrates on the subsidiary step, and he evolves the sentence:

Fatigue is more a matter of atmosphere than of hours.

This sentence he also memorises, and again notes points to remember:

*tiredness makes staff susceptible to colds and 'flu

*tiredness causes irritability, quarrels, less work

*tiredness causes headaches.

To recap, the main sentence is:

You can turn an eight hour day into an eight hour working day,

and the subsidiary sentence:

Fatigue is more a matter of atmosphere than of hours.

These will be the sentences to be memorised, and

expanded upon according to a prospect's needs, but there is still more work to be done before the presentation can be finalised.

'YES' RESPONSES

Making statements, however good they may be, is not good salesmanship.

Why?

Because we do not know:

(a) if the prospect has heard us

(b) if he has understood us

(c) if he agrees with us.

We, therefore, have to adopt a technique of making positive statements, and asking positive questions which will evoke 'yes' responses. When we have our prospect's agreement, we know that we can continue with our presentation.

The telephone salesman will, therefore, prepare a number of questions to which he is certain of getting 'yes' response.

'Mr. Brown, the number of air changes required in an office varies from two to four. You would like to have instant control of those air changes, wouldn't you?'

'Yes.'

'One popular feature of our units is the variable control. At full speed you will remove 41,000 cubic feet of air per hour, *which means that* you will still have perfect conditions even when the fan is operating against a head wind. Mr. Brown, at the moment when you want to ventilate the office you have to open the windows, is that right?'

'Yes.'

'And Mr. Brown, when the window is open isn't it draughty for the girls working at desks near the window?'

'Yes, we have had complaints.'

'Well, there will be no draughts when our unit is installed, *which means that* you will be able to place desks right alongside the windows if necessary. You would like to make use of that extra floorspace, wouldn't you?'

'Yes, it would help.'

'By the way, Mr. Brown, I am sure you will agree that *fatigue is often more a matter of atmosphere than of hours*. That is why staff tend to ease off during the afternoon. We all feel drowsy in a stuffy atmosphere, don't we?'

'Yes, I suppose we do.'

'The unit will circulate the air when necessary, extract air, or bring air in. It will prove its worth during the winter and the summer, because research has shown that good air conditioning is one of the sure ways of cutting down absenteeism, *which means that* you won't be spending money paying out wages to staff who are ill in bed with flu and colds.'

In giving these examples of 'yes' responses the customer's agreement has been obtained after each question. This does not always happen. He could raise an objection, and objections will be dealt with in a later chapter. But when the objection is answered, the telephone salesman must obtain the 'yes' response, to be sure that the prospect is satisfied. This presentation is based on the day to day work of a salesman in this field, telephoning in response to an enquiry, the prospect having had all the relevant data regarding size, price, and fixing.

Here are the kind of questions which can be asked by salesmen working in other spheres:

'You do agree that advertising on the packet is good advertising, don't you, Mr. Smith?'

'You would like to increase your profit margin, wouldn't you, Mr. White?'

'If you could cut costs by 5% right away you would want to start immediately, wouldn't you?'

'Mr. Brown, you wouldn't like to take any risks for one day longer than you need, so I am sure you would like to be covered right away, wouldn't you?'

'You do risk losing custom when you are out of stock, don't you?'

'A series of advertisements would bring far better results against cost, I am sure you agree with that, Mr. Johnson. . . .'

To Remind You

When building a presentation:

1. Use golden words – expressive words
2. Know your product – know your market
3. Keep to the sequence

    The Approach
    Main Benefit
    Subsidiary Benefit } Create Confidence
    Close

4. Base the approach on a compelling reason for the buyer to listen to you.
5. Remember to turn needs into *wants*.
6. Base benefits on buying reasons.

7. Analyse products to find buying reasons and benefits.
8. Evolve and memorise selling sentences to remind you of complete step.

which means that you will be able to move smoothly into the close.

CLOSING THE SALE

Often a play or musical fails on opening in a London theatre after a provincial run. Then the excuses flow from the producer, director, actors and actresses – 'We opened at the wrong time' – 'The weather was against us' – 'The critics panned us unfairly' – 'We were affected by the strike. . . .'

These excuses make no allowance for the fact that other shows manage to carry on in spite of these difficulties.

When a production fails the reason can usually be traced to mistakes in judgement. The playwright, would not accept changes – others involved refused to accept criticism – the actors and actresses were badly cast. . . . Problems during the provincial run were waved aside as being of no consequence – 'It will be all right on the night!' But the show was doomed to failure from the beginning. Would the playwright ever admit this? Would the actor agree that he was inaudible to the back row? Would the producer believe that the play which had a special message couldn't find an audience who wanted to listen to that message?

The failure was not due to any sudden change in the weather, or a strike, or even because the critics panned it. Many shows have succeeded in spite of such criticism. The play failed way back.

It is very similar to a sale. Sales are never lost at the last moment. The mistakes are made much earlier. All telephone salesmen should write on a card:

I do not lose orders because of my weak closing techniques.
I lose orders because my presentation is not good enough.

That is the first lesson to be learned if more orders are to be obtained. The old selling axiom that *a good sale closes itself* is still true. Sometimes, however, a buyer, even although he is well sold, is still hesitant, and there are many ways of nudging the buyer into saying, 'I'll go ahead.'

What is meant by the *professional* salesman is a question I am often asked. Is a man of fifty, after thirty years on the road, a truly professional salesman, while the man with only three years' experience is an amateur?

Not at all. Some amateurs are old time salesmen who believe that they are fully experienced because of the time they have spent facing customers. How about the dynamic young man? The quick-witted, fast talker – he could also be an amateur, although he is sure that he is a professional.

The professional salesman:

(a) learns from experience. He does believe that by the act of calling on customers he is necessarily gaining experience in salesmanship. He knows that experience comes from analysing the calls, pinpointing mistakes, and assessing the need for change.

(b) is interested in his work and is always eager to improve his selling skills. He knows that only a

genius can break fundamental rules in salesmanship or sport, and succeed. He also knows there
are not many geniuses about.

Unfortunately, amateur salesmen believe they are
endowed with special qualities, and that they can
break the rules or even not bother to learn the rules,
and still succeed.

The telephone salesman must also learn the fundamentals of telephone selling and become truly professional by applying them.

Here are some basic rules for closing orders:

1. There must be no attempt to close an order until
   you are certain that your prospect understands your
   proposition. Orders closed too quickly lead to
   cancellations. The exception is when a prospect
   understands his requirements, and expresses his
   willingness to buy. For example, he might say, 'I
   know all about it and have been considering the
   idea for some time. I suppose I should have made up
   my mind. . . .' That prospect knows what he wants,
   and the salesman must close the order.

2. You must always ask for the order, but if you fail,
   you must leave the door open so that your next call
   will be welcome. On making your second call, be
   positive and assume that the decision is in your
   favour. Never ask, 'Have you made up your mind?'
   Take up a point from the previous call and continue from that point:

   'Mr. Brown, when I spoke to you yesterday you
   were concerned that our prices were more expensive than our main competitor. Well, Mr. Brown,
   I have given this serious thought. They could
   probably reduce their prices even further. The

fact that we are unable to do so proves to you not only the quality of our product, but its saleability. After all, our products have been succeeding for over twenty years. . . .'

3. When the order is closed the salesman must ring off quickly, after a sentence to cement confidence:

'I'll telephone you again when it is delivered.'

'I'll make sure it is delivered on time.'

'You will be delighted when it is installed.'

4. When selling consumer goods the salesman will close quickly on each line as it is offered.

5. Assume that the order is yours from the very first words of the approach. This positiveness on your part will come through over the telephone early in the presentation. Use such explicit statements as:

'You can telephone me personally if ever you require service.'

'You will like the chair because of its appearance, but most of all because of its comfort when you sit down in the evenings.'

'Your advertisement will have tremendous appeal and will get a sure response. . . .'

6. *Buying Signals*

The telephone salesman must be brief and must always close if he receives a buying signal when the presentation is nearing its conclusion. The prospect may say:

'Do you find they are selling well?'

'Can you deliver quickly?'

'What did you say the measurements are?'

'Will it help to avoid. . . .'

'You did say I should have exclusive rights for a month?'

'What are your credit terms?'

'Will I have any problem in obtaining spares?'

These are definite buying signals. Listen to them. They prove that the prospect is sold and it is only a question of asking for the order.

HOW TO ASK

The direct request can be made:

'May I write the order up?'

'I take it that you want one.'

'Will you give me the order?'

You might win, but you might precipitate the clicking of the receiver as it is placed back on the cradle. The prospect's 'NO' is so final.

Far better than putting a direct question is to offer the prospect alternatives.

'Would you prefer a gross or two gross with the special discount?'

'It could be installed in the window facing south or the one facing east. Which is your preference?'

'Would you prefer our cleaning staff to arrive early in the morning or after you have closed in the evenings?'

If, to any of these alternatives, an indecisive reply is received, the salesman has still not lost the order, or command of the situation. He can continue selling.

Research has shown that 74% of all telephone salesmen use the *alternative* as a closing aid. Often, however, the *alternative close* is linked with other methods of finalising the presentation. These can be closes within their own right, but when the buyer needs an extra nudge, use the *alternative close*.

These are proved closing techniques:

Concession Close

When selling consumer goods, special promotions and concessions are usually part of the sales presentation. There are occasions, when a salesman is allowed to grant a concession which is not applicable to all of his customers; extra discount, longer credit, special deliveries, thirteen for twelve, a free service, a refund guarantee. . . .

Many telephone salesmen give the concession at the approach but this is wrong. The rule is: *sell as if you did not have the concession*. The order might close easily and you have no need to give away some of your company's profits. It is when the order is proving difficult to close that the concession can have real weight.

The Summary Close

In telephone selling the presentation is so short that the majority of prospects will retain the main points in their mind, but there is always the buyer who only half listens and even gives 'yes' responses, automatically.

For those buyers, the telephone salesman summarises the main features and benefits of his product and then asks for the order.

The Summary Close is sometimes call the *reminder* close.

The Fear Close

It is used by salesmen selling fire extinguishers, burglar alarms, safes, insurance, and many other products and services. The telephone salesman selling consumer or consumer durables can sometimes use it when (a) the customer is afraid of running out of stock during a busy time, or (b) a competitor will obtain preferential support.

Used judiciously, the fear close can activate the prospect who hesitates to place an order for capital equipment, or to stock a new line.

The Verbal Proof Story Close

This close is similar to the *reference approach*. It is a confidence builder, and can prove most helpful when selling to a timid buyer.

The telephone salesman concludes his presentation with a success story. A telephone salesman selling advertising space to the owner of a TV and radio store might say:

'Mr. Brown, you do know Pickles of Wrexton, don't you . . . ?'

'Yes, they are well known in the trade.'

'So are you, Mr. Brown, but I think it will interest you to hear that Mr. Pickles was very hesitant about taking space in our magazine. Like you he thought the local press would be better for him. Also, he wanted to cut down on his advertising expenditure, not increase it. But he decided to take a full page, and the response was so good that he has now booked a whole series. You would find the same would happen to you, Mr. Brown. . . .'

The rule applying to the verbal proof story is that it must be true, and applicable, and relating to a business away from the locality in which the prospect is situated.

Closing on a Minor Point

This is part *Assumptive Close* and part *Alternative Close*. The telephone salesman will say:

'You do agree, Mr. Brown, that you prefer a remote control with the unit, don't you?'

'Mr. Smith, we deliver Thursday, would that be all right for you?'

'As it is a present, Mr. Jones, would you like it specially gift wrapped?'

The telephone salesman must assume that if the prospect agrees on the minor point he is ready to place the order.

The Isolation Close

The telephone salesman separates the one point that is holding up the order. He ignores irrelevant differences and says firmly:

'Mr. Brown, the single point which makes you hesitate is that you believe that our minimum order is too large for you. Let me put this in its right perspective: I should be letting you down if I supplied you with less than our minimum, because you would not be able to satisfy the demand, and we couldn't deliver a fresh supply to you in time. . . .'

'All that separates us, Mr. Jones, is that you need extended credit facilities. This is what we can do to help you. . . .'

CLOSE THAT ORDER

It is always fear which stops prospects from buying – fear of making a mistake, fear of reprimand from higher authority, fear of spending too much money, fear of loss of security, fear of what his wife (or her husband) will say, fear of over-stocking, fear of being talked into an order. . . .

You must calm their fears by closing in a positive manner. Until the sale is closed the salesman is a conversationalist. Only when the order is finalised is he a salesman.

CHAPTER 4

Your Voice is Your Selling Personality

Although the telephone salesman has the disadvantage of being unable to use visual aids, he has the advantage of not being in a position to distract a buyer. During face to face selling, mannerisms can be sales losers. A salesman may pick a spot on his face, jingle his keys, play with a pen, or do an off-and-on act with his glasses. If he has a cold he may sneeze and blow his nose every few seconds. The telephone salesman can indulge his mannerisms without necessarily impairing his sales presentation. He knows that he sells by the words he uses and the personality of his voice.

A lack-lustre voice can have the same effect on a buyer as a salesman's lethargic expression when selling face to face. For your presentation to be 100% effective, for your listener to warm to you over the telephone, and more important, to hear and understand every word of your sales sequence, you must have a telephone voice of good quality.

But that is the problem. We all think we have a good voice – it is a part of us, the way we are made. . . .

Or is it? Unless there is some deformity, everyone has similar vocal chords, diaphragm, and tongue. We are not born with round shoulders, we develop them from a bad stance. We are not born without the ability to smile. Some people smile more than others as they mature. So it is with the voice. Speaking is an imitative faculty. Our speech, generally, is a result of birthplace, upbringing, and association with others. By the time we reach our twenties the voice we use is finalised. If,

59

however, we have the determination, we are able to improve it in the same way as we can straighten our backs.

It has so often been said that you cannot change people. The comment may be made in reference to someone's meanness, selfishness, hardness, or lack of common sense. In such cases people rarely do change as they live out their lives. Others may suffer from psychological problems – irrational fears, timidity, arrogance, or a propensity to lie. Psychiatrists can sometimes eradicate these traits.

Sales tuition does not set out to change people, but to increase their natural attributes. Anyone unhappy about the sound of his voice or diction can, by effort and determination, put matters right.

In business we are expected to speak acceptably to our customers, and the telephone salesman most of all must remember the voice, that wonderful instrument he uses when shaping and making words.

VOICE PRODUCTION

Voice production is based on good breathing. Good breathing means correct breathing. Correct breathing means controlled breathing, or taking in the right amount of breath at the right place, and using it in order to give the right motive power which makes for voice quality.

Everyone has the machinery for this control. When that machinery is not used properly we lack breath, resulting in irregular rhythm and poor voice quality. Most people, when attempting to put more power in their voice, think of their vocal chords. This only causes tension in the muscles surrounding the vocal chords resulting in a dry wheezy tone of voice. To improve your voice quality you must forget your vocal chords and concentrate on your lungs. You will then have taken your first step towards diaphragmatic breathing.

Unfortunately, natural breathing sometimes means taking in only shallow breaths. If we are called upon to make a speech this results in quickly running out of breath, perhaps feeling unwell, or just managing to stutter and stammer our way through the ordeal.

When we sell, either face to face or over the telephone, we have to maintain voice power and voice quality, to communicate effectively. This can only be brought about by correct breathing.

Test 1

Place the palm of your hand firmly on that V-shape in the breastbone just below the rib. You can now feel the diaphragm working gently. Next, imagine that you have just raced round the block and you are puffing hard – puff. Now you can feel the diaphragm working really hard.

This is what is happening: As you inhale, your lungs expand pushing the elastic diaphragm down and out. As you exhale, in and up goes the diaphragm, resulting in more rapid propulsion of the outgoing air passing over the vocal chords.

When speaking, you inhale more rapidly and exhale more slowly. This enables you to conserve your breath to make words and sentences.

Test 2

Imagine that you have just enjoyed a wonderful meal

prepared by a cordon bleu chef, with specially selected vintage wines, you have been the guest of honour and your virtues have been extolled. Having made your speech, and received warm and generous applause, you sit back in your chair feeling that all is well with the world.

You sigh, a deep sigh of repletion and contentment. Have you got the picture? Right, now sigh. Sigh deeply. Once more. How deeply you breathed. And that sigh exercise is basically all that you need to know about breath replenishment.

Test 3

All breath, to be correctly used, should enter through the nostrils to filter and warm it, but occasionally this can be noisy and not instantaneous in its effect. For silence and efficiency, therefore, breath may be taken in through a slightly open mouth.

Now breathe in through your mouth while it is only slightly open. When you reach what you believe to be the absolute limit of expansion of the diaphragm, take in a little more breath, and there will be more expansion. Then try once more. You will be surprised to learn that nearly always there is some room left for expansion. Conversely, when you believe that you have emptied your lungs of air, there is nearly always some breath left in the lungs, some energy left in the diaphragm to give the air that extra propulsion. This should teach you that you have the ability to speak, when necessary, long sentences without taking breath, resulting in a smooth vocal tone, without jerkiness.

EXERCISES

The following exercises will help you to gain effective breath control:

Exercise 1
To ease throat muscular tension sit in a chair and relax head and shoulders. Allow first your left shoulder, and then your right shoulder to slump towards your chest, with arms falling between your legs. Roll your head forward on to the chest, breathe deeply six times saying to yourself, 'Let go – let go. . . .' The word *let* as you breathe in, and *go* as you breathe out.

Exercise 2
Stand in front of a mirror and breathe in deeply and out slowly. The mirror is to enable you to make certain that you are not lifting your shoulders. Most people lift their shoulders up as they breathe deeply, and this action does not help your breathing at all. As you breathe in, count five, increasing this daily until you can reach eight. Count ten as you start to breathe out, and increase this until you reach twenty or more. Repeat this exercise six times. You will not need to take such deep breaths when speaking normally, but this exercise will help you to develop your breath control.

Exercise 3
Mark off in a book several medium to long sentences, and read these sentences aloud in one breath.

Exercise 4
To maintain correct breathing, but to put a lilt in your voice, carry out the following exercise:

Sing a snatch of a song, e.g. 'Won't you come home Bill Bailey, Land of Hope and Glory, or any popular modern melody.

Sing the line three times, then stop. Say the words once more, but without taking breath, repeating the words in your normal speaking voice. This will help to make your voice mellow and tuneful. You will find that subsequent to your singing the refrain you will not be able to drop into a flat conversational style.

Exercise 5
For three minutes each morning practise reading aloud from a book. Your rhythm will depend on your breathing. This will enable you to speak rythmically.

FORMING WORDS

'He's tongue-tied.' When we say that we usually mean that someone doesn't communicate well. But speakers in every category are often tongue-tied in a different sense. They do not realise that the tongue is meant to move into position in order to establish sounds accurately. A virile tongue must work in conjunction with a mobile jaw, to give clarity to the words we use. Few speakers open their mouths sufficiently. This must result in an imperfect and muffled tone. You cannot speak effectively through half-closed lips.

Exercise 1
(a) Yawn. That's easy, isn't it? Yawn six times. This will help you to have a more mobile jaw.
(b) Repeat six times *you*, *why*, and *Yokohama*, exaggerating each word as you say it. Carry out this exercise morning and evening.

Exercise 2

(a) So that your tongue can become more mobile place a finger in front of your mouth, about one inch away. Try to touch the finger with your tongue.

(b) Move the finger a little further away and try again.

(c) Keep the tongue straight, then try imitating a snake by flicking out your tongue, and try to reach the finger.

(d) Try to touch the tip of your nose with your tongue. Repeat these exercises six times.

GOOD DICTION

Many a time you must have wondered if your hearing was impaired when listening to an after-dinner speaker. Only good manners prohibit you from shouting, 'I can't hear what you are saying'.

We now know that this lack of clarity can be due to many factors. It can happen, however, even when a speaker is shouting, because the outline of his words may be blurred.

This can be corrected by the better use of certain sounds – consonants, they are called. Sounds like P T D CH K L M N give greater emphasis, and sharper authority to the words we use.

Have you heard of *Slurvian*? Another Ruritanian kingdom? Not at all! It is the language of those who slur their words. Here are some examples:

Lazn'genlmn	instead of	ladies and gentle-men
awnjuice	instead of	orange juice
azamarrafac'	instead of	as a matter of fact

The *t*'s have disappeared, and also a *d* in the first example, and an *r* in the second.

Slurvian must be avoided at all costs by the telephone salesman. Here are some more examples:

baddle for battle
liddle for little
boddle for bottle
fordy for forty
kep' for kept
cruss for crusts
twen'y for twenty

Exercises

Speak *Slurvian* in front of a mirror and then correct yourself. You will be able to watch your mouth and notice how much more active your tongue is in the correct pronunciation.

THE VOWELS

The consonants are standard, but vowel sounds can change the type of speech we use. We all remember a, e, i, o, u, but, of course, there are many other vowel sounds as well. Effective vowel use is achieved by the elasticity of the lips. Without this flexibility we are apt to say *terdye* instead of *today*, *feller* instead of *fellow*, and *ejicate* instead of *educate*.

Exercise 1

In front of a mirror whisper a, e, i, o, u. Can you see your lips moving? Repeat a little louder, watching for the lip movements. Shout out the sounds. Now you can see your lips moving. Next mouth the vowels without making a sound. Exaggerate the effort. Watch for lip movements the whole time.

Repeat this exercise six times.

EMPHASIS

Very quickly most people tire of listening. When talking to a buyer this can result in the loss of a sale. We must, therefore, make sure that the sound of our words is more compelling. This means taking one word in a group of words, and emphasising it. By so doing we may change the meaning. For example, we can say, 'Thank you very much,' as a flat disinterested piece of pseudo courtesy, or we can say, 'Thank you *very* much.' This is much more personal.

The same applies to single words. 'No' can have many different meaning. Say 'No' to yourself now. It could mean a refusal, but put life in your voice and the *no* expresses surprise. Change the sound again and you can convey sympathy.

Coupled with emphasis is inflection, the tone in the voice as it has sometimes been called. A buyer will listen more intently if he hears a variety of sounds. For example, 'Will you be in your office in the morning?' can sound flat and uninteresting, but if you begin the 'Will you' on a high note, dropping to a lower tone at 'in the morning' you will have given light and shade to the whole sentence.

You can also emphasise syllables in words, almost putting them to music. You can say, 'It is exquisite,' meaning you are pleased with a design, but emphasise the *ex* or the *qui* and then you mean that the design is gorgeous.

BETTER COMMUNICATION

The professional telephone salesman will study this chapter and immediately set about checking his voice and, if necessary, improving it. The amateur will not bother, believing that everyone understands every word he says. However monotonous his voice may be, he will believe it to be strong and resonant, forgetting that for the telephone salesman his voice is his main selling instrument.

No professional would play golf with a broken club. No snooker champion would use a bent cue. No telephone salesman should sell with a voice that might impair the satisfactory conclusion of a sale.

There is a need for precision and quality in telephone selling if misunderstandings are to be avoided.

Your voice will register your mood, and your mood when telephone selling, must always be cheerful. Your enthusiasm must radiate over the wires. You are concerned with presenting your personality in words. Colourful delivery is the expression of personality, and an expression of a vibrant personality is always good salesmanship.

CHAPTER 5

How to get Appointments by Telephone

The salesman's profitable time is the time he spends face to face with his customers and, of course, prospects, because few salesmen have all the customers they can handle. Most salesmen, therefore, while obtaining the maximum amount of business from their customers, must also seek out prospects to turn them into future customers.

In the industrial market, and even in the consumer field when contacting chain stores, he faces a problem: How to see those prospects who do not want to see him. Usually, his customers will see him. If they won't, then he has failed in his relationship with them, or something is wrong with his company's products. But obtaining an interview with a prospect needs a different technique from knocking on the door of one of his regular buyers.

What are his alternatives? He can call cold, or make an appointment by telephone.

Even if he is given enquiries to follow up, he will, more often than not, have to telephone for an appointment.

Cold calling will always have its place in selling and in some forms of marketing it is essential, but it is usually a fill-in for the industrial salesman. Rather than waste time between appointments, he will call cold on any nearby prospects. But cold calling as a planned system of working can be very time consuming. For example, there can be long waits in reception areas until the prospect is disengaged. Also, a full day's work may result in only two good interviews, but telephoning in advance may enable a salesman to make four or five appointments a day.

Preparation

The basis of all telephone selling – and making appointments by telephone is hard selling – must be good preparation. There are several rules to follow before making an appointment by telephone, and one golden rule: *you must find out the prospect's name.*

Knowing the prospect's name will help you to handle his telephone operator, and by addressing your prospect by name you are able to bring immediate warmth to the relationship with him.

It is important to use a name in selling face to face, but it is even more vital when trying to win a prospect over during a few minutes' telephone conversation. If all else fails and you cannot discover the prospect's name, then you must telephone his receptionist, ask her for the name of the works manager (or whoever it is you want to speak to) thank her, and ring off; because at this stage, if you ask to be put through you may be questioned. You should then telephone again the next day.

The other rules are:

(a) You must have customer files available and prospect information cards. The customer files or prospect cards are important because they may contain information allowing you to anticipate a customer or prospect's reaction.

(b) A customer may have had a delivery complaint. A prospect might not have purchased previously because he considered the price too high. With this knowledge available you can forestall an objection to the interview.

(c) Directories, brochures, and any other information which you may need should be at hand. The names and telephone numbers of calls you intend making will be listed in front of you and, of course, pen and paper to make notes.

(d) Your diary is invaluable to you. Whenever possible you will suggest days and times for the appointments to suit your convenience. Good appointment planning will leave time for cold calling on nearby prospects, or may even completely fill the day with appointments. You can only achieve these results by constant reference to your diary.

(e) Make sure that you will not be disturbed while telephoning. The emphasis is on *you*. You must never ask a secretary or telephone operator to get the prospect on the line for you.

Now, are you ready?

Making the Call
Pick up the telephone, dial the number, and on being greeted by the telephone operator, ask to speak to Mr. Smith.

One of three things can happen:

(a) The operator will transfer you immediately to Mr. Smith and all will be well.

(b) The operator may ask you your business.

(c) The operator may put you through to Mr. Smith's secretary.

To avoid (b) and (c) you must have an authoritative approach.

'Will you please tell Mr. Smith your financial

director that John White is on the line for him. Thank you.'

The *John* personalises the approach. Never use the prefix Mr. The *thank you* gives it a finality which does not invite a response. Unless the telephone operator has special screening instructions regarding incoming calls, you will be put through to Mr. Smith.

Now we come to (b). The operator asks you for further information. You answer, quite simply:

'It is a business matter.'

Don't add anything further. It is not a misleading statement, because it is a business matter which you can discuss only with Mr. Smith the financial director.

Alternatively, it will show equal authority if you imply that you wish to discuss something of great importance. For example:

'It is in connection with Mr. Smith's financial planning.'

There is an excellent third approach if a letter has been sent in advance to the prospect, either a personal letter or a DMA shot. You would then say:

'It is with reference to the letter I wrote him.'

If the operator has been instructed to insist on obtaining information from every caller asking for Mr. Smith you must then say:

'I am sorry, but it is a very involved matter. I think it would be best if you put me through to Mr. Smith's secretary.'

It is sometimes advisable when making appointments to ask for a secretary in the first place, but in the main it is better to ask for the executive concerned. The secretary may be away or out of her office, and in this event the operator *may* put you straight through to the man you want to contact. If you do speak to the secretary, however, either by your own request or because the operator has instructions, you will then have the selling task of persuading her to make an appointment for you to see Mr. Smith. You will use the selling principles outlined in the Telephone Sales Presentation, plus the golden words:

'I would like to ask your advice.'

You will not win every time, but you will win far more often than you will lose. In the majority of cases you will, therefore, be able to speak to Mr. Smith.

What do you say to him?

The Hinge

There should, whenever possible, be a hinge on which to hang your approach. This can be a letter which you or your company may have written, an advertisement, something new, a commercial on TV, a window display, or a reference from a friend or business associate. Your approach could be:

'Mr. Smith, this is John White of the Bridgewater Machine Tool Company. Have you a moment to speak on the telephone?'

This courtesy request, 'Have you a moment . . .' is not laid down as a fixed rule. It can, however, be very effective. It relaxes the prospect, because you have only asked him for a moment of his time. Also, it shows a courtesy that is lacking in so many telephone calls.

Whether you use this sentence or not, you must now repeat the prospect's name, after you have given him the name of your company.

Letter hinge

'Mr. Smith, did you receive my letter?'

'No, what was it about?'

'Mr. Smith, it was about your car. . . .'

Another example

'Mr. Smith, did you receive my letter?'

'About your car washing system, wasn't it?'

'That's right. I want to call to see you, to explain. . . .'

Advertisement hinge

'Mr. Smith, did you see our advertisement in The Engineering News, announcing our new checking device which could help you so much to reduce costs. . . .'

Reference hinge

'Mr. Smith, we haven't met, but John Williams asked me to contact you. . . .'

The Quick Approach Close

In all forms of selling it is axiomatic that a salesman should think of the close the minute the sale begins, but in telephone selling there is a difference. You can actually close at the approach. The prospect might be influenced by the name of your company, or interested in the product or service you are selling, or he likes the sound of your voice – you sound like someone he should listen to – or it may even be that he is very busy and arrives at a quick decision. Whatever the reason, this form of approach does get appointments. This is how to do it:

With conviction in your voice to create the impression that there cannot be a refusal you say:

'Good morning Mr. Jones, this is Jack Smith of Halliday publications. I should like to take up just eight minutes of your time to tell you about our new journal for your industry and its wonderful advertising pull. Would Wednesday morning or Wednesday afternoon be more convenient for me to call?'

This approach covers a lot if ground. It is brief. It asks for only a short interview. It states your business; and it closes.

The Question Hinge
When you haven't a hinge of any kind, then ask a question:

Mr. Smith, this is Mike Boon of the Bessing Group. Have you heard of our organisation?'

Whether you receive the reply 'yes' or 'no' is immaterial, because it will take you smoothly in to the main reason for your call.

Be Special
A wonderful word to use in all approaches is *special*, or *specially* –

'Mr. Smith, I am calling you *specially* to tell you about. . . .'

'Mr. Jones, there is a *special* reason why I should like to see you. . . .'

Keep to the Rules
Although the quick close will get you interviews, in many cases there will be a request for further information. Here are some points to remember:

Time is not on your side, so keep the benefit short.

You must not become involved in a full presentation.

Keep the objective in mind: *to obtain an interview*.

You must use short sentences.

You must use understandable words.

You must be authoritative, but never talk down to the prospect.

You must not try to be too clever. You have to persuade the prospect that you are a sincere person by the words you use, and by the tone of your voice.

You must have a reason for not giving full information over the telephone, e.g. samples to be shown, a model of a building to examine, figures to analyse, a drawing to discuss, or matters so personal that they should be discussed face to face.

You may also have to evaluate the prospect, if his buying potential is not known. It is time wasting to make an appointment with a prospect who seems interested in office partitioning if his offices are small, brick built, and he is not allowed by his landlord to knock down the walls. If you are selling a property trust bond plus insurance, and to make the policy worthwhile the prospect has to invest a minimum of £1000, then you will have to discover whether he has this cash available.

Evaluation is best carried out when the prospect has shown interest in your proposal, and you know you will get an appointment. You then use the question technique.

The salesman selling partitioning could say,

'Can you tell me the approximate size of your main office?'

The insurance salesman may be quite direct:

'Mr. Smith, if you were shown how you could add 50% to your capital, are you prepared to put down £1000?'

You can always back out of an interview by saying, 'Mr. Smith, perhaps I had better send you literature first.'

The telephone salesman will only withdraw from the interview if he is certain the customer either cannot afford his product or service, or, within the foreseeable future, will not be in the market for it.

The Main Benefit

You must stake your claim for an interview in a few compelling words:

'I'd like to show you some recent information on. . . .'

'You will want to consider six ideas for cutting down overheads in your offices. . . .'

'We have designed a very unusual saving plan which will be of great benefit to you. . . .'

'The mighty midget office copier is no bigger than your desk pad. Knowing something of your company's activities, you would find this of tremendous help for personal use. . . .'

'You would want to handle the stitcher yourself, to see how well it works. . . .'

Your aim is to intrigue the prospect, to interest him so that he will want to hear more and will give you an interview.

The Objections

What could his objections be? He can hardly object to your product or service, because you have only given him the barest outline. He can only object to you taking up his time at an interview.

What can happen? He can answer:

'I'll see you,' and all will be well.

'Send me the information.'

'Tell me now.'

'I'm too busy.'

There are several ways of tackling the request for further information.

'Mr. Smith, you would want to see proof of how a company has been able to increase overall production by up to 28%.'

'What I want to talk to you about, Mr. Brown, is details of a new way in which you can protect your money and beat inflation. Would next Tuesday morning. . . .'

'Mr. Jones, you demand a very fast delivery service. We can provide that at low cost, and you will want to examine this claim. It is for this reason that I want the opportunity of meeting you. May I call. . . .'

'I cannot advise you, Mr. Black, until I know one or two things about your company. . . .'

'You would need to look at our analysis forms, Mr. Clark, I'll bring them with me. It will only take a few minutes. May I call on. . . .'

To the statement, 'I am too busy' the salesman has several answers, according to what he is selling.

'That is why I am telephoning you, Mr. Smith, because I know you are so busy. I can help you in this direction by cutting down some of the demands on your time.'

Ego building can also be a sound policy.

'Mr. White, I have found that it is the busy people like you who are most interested. . . .'

Or assume that the prospect is only encountering a temporary rush of business.

'Of course, Mr. Howell, I know how busy you are, I

was not thinking of disturbing you today or tomorrow. Will you be able to see me on Thursday or Friday of next week. . . .'

If he still persists that he is busy, then an unusual request could be made:

'It is because you are so busy that I feel my proposition will have real value for you. Perhaps I can help you personally. May I call to see you outside business hours? Either early in the morning, or later in the evening – say six o'clock or seven – which would you prefer?'

Surprisingly, this unusual request is very often quite acceptable. If you do see the prospect after office hours you will find him more relaxed and receptive to your ideas than when he is involved in the rush and bustle of a busy office.

If you reach a point where you feel you are antagonising the prospect, then you must never shut the door to a future appointment.

'I'll call you again in a fortnight's time, Mr. Smith.'

If this does not work there is always one final request which you can make. It is rarely refused:

'Mr. Smith, there are some times of the day when you are not so busy as others, although I appreciate that you cannot specify them. When I am near your offices, may I call on the off-chance of seeing you?'

He will nearly always say 'yes' and this is noted in your cold calling diary.

Following the telephone call, after two or three visits at the most, you will find that you will see Mr. Smith.

The Close

Tying up an appointment is different from locking up

an order, when you can use any of the closes set out in the sales presentation. This is not possible when selling the interview. Nearly always, therefore, you will use the Alternative Close, based on an appointment time.

Most salesmen suggest a time for a meeting on the hour or the half-hour. You can be different. Put forward 9–10 a.m. or 3.50 p.m. The very unexpected nature of this suggestion will often bring its own reward. But the main reason for using this technique is that many busy people make appointments on the hour or half-hour, some of which will last for the full period, and others will be cut short. The odd time, therefore, will often appeal to the prospect whose appointments on the hour may leave him periods in between which are free.

And remember, you are only asking for a few minutes of his time, knowing that if you interest him, he will ask you to remain.

Another factor adds value to the odd-time appointment: it indicates to the prospect that you are a busy person, and that you are fitting him into your full day's schedule of appointments.

The Close, therefore, can be:

'Will Wednesday or Thursday suit you best, Mr. Lovell?'

'Er – Wednesday.'

'Morning or afternoon?'

'Afternoon is best for me.'

'That's fine, Mr. Lovell. Then can you make it two-ten, or would four-fifty be more convenient?'

'Ten past two would suit me.'

'Thank you, Mr. Lovell, I'll look forward to being with you at ten past two on Wednesday.'

Keep on Closing

Do you remember the story of the old-time salesman who kept seven coins in his pocket? At every refusal to buy he would transfer one coin to another pocket. If he had not got the order by the time the seventh coin had been moved he would pack up and go.

He claimed that he rarely had to take more than four or five coins away, even when selling to the most difficult customers, but he believed in the salesman's creed, *never give up, keep trying*.

In telephone selling there isn't the time to ask for the order seven times, but you can ask two or three times. This is how it is done:

Example A

The following technique shows how an insurance salesman can keep asking for an appointment:

'Good morning, Mr. Swift, my name is Jack Barclay of The World-Wide Insurance Company. I should like to take up just nine minutes of your time to tell you about our Executive Plan. Would Tuesday morning next, or Thursday afternoon at 2.50 p.m. be more convenient?'

'What's it all about?'

'Mr. Swift, it's to show you how you can increase your capital – a fascinating subject, I'm sure you will agree. Would Tuesday morning or Thursday. . . .' (first trial close).

'You want to sell me insurance?'

'Are you interested in insurance?'

'No.'

'What I want to talk about, Mr. Swift, is a new way you can protect your money and beat inflation.

Would Tuesday morning. . . .' (second trial close).

'I haven't any money to invest.'

'Mr. Swift, all I am asking you to invest is nine minutes of your time. Would Tuesday morning. . . .' (third trial close).

More often than not the appointment will be given after the first, second, or third close. One golden rule to observe is: *keep command of the conversation*. If the prospect takes charge you will lose the interview.

Here is another variation of this presentation:

'Good morning, Mr. Swift, my name is Jack Barclay of The World-Wide Insurance Company. I should like to take up just nine minutes of your time to tell you about our Executive Plan. Would Tuesday morning next or Thursday afternoon at 2.50 p.m. be more convenient?'

'I'm not interested.'

'Mr. Swift, I realise that you will not be interested until I have told you about the Executive Plan. Would Tuesday morning or Thursday afternoon at 2.50 p.m. be more convenient?'

'I haven't time to discuss personal matters at my office, I'm far too busy.'

'Mr. Swift, may I ask you a question? Like most people today you save money in one way or another, don't you?'

'Well, yes.'

'Good. Now if there were a scheme available that gave you a higher return for your money than your present saving plan, you would want to know about it, wouldn't you?'

'Of course.'

'Fine! That is just what I want to talk to you about.

Now would Tuesday morning. . . .'

The technique of asking a question and diverting attention from the objection is a good technique for obtaining an appointment.

Example B
(The salesman of Arrow Weighing Machine Company is telephoning a Works Director, seeking an appointment.)

'Mr. Harvey? Good morning, this is Peter Lisle of The Arrow Weighing Machine Company. We met some three years ago when the maintenance contract on your weighing equipment was arranged. Can you spare me a moment?'

'Yes.'

'Mr. Harvey, the contract is due for renewal next month. You will want to see the new proposal, may I call on Wednesday. . .?'

'There's no need for you to come here. You can post the papers on to me.'

'Thank you, Mr. Harvey, but reports from my engineers show that certain machines are being used either less or more than they were three years ago. You will agree that we should try to get the frequency of maintenance on each machine in relation to its use and importance. On Wednesday I can explain. . . .'

'You'd be better talking to my chief engineer about this. He'll know what he wants, and I will accept his recommendations, provided the charge for the contract isn't any higher than before. Costs seem to keep rising.'

'They do indeed, Mr. Harvey, and you'll understand

that in providing a service, a very high proportion of the premium is directly related to labour costs – and we both know how wages keep going up. In any event, you and I can work this out between us, and I'm sure you'll agree that we should have a talk about it. Would Wednesday. . .?'

Particular Points

1. Reason for call made clear. Mr. Harvey *might* have agreed to see the salesman without more discussion.
2. A valid, although secondary reason for wanting an appointment.
3. The primary reason comes out but is not dealt with as Peter Lisle does not want to become involved in a price discussion. The need for the meeting is brought to a 'you and I' situation. Lisle has raised the importance of the issue, and has built up the ego of Mr. Harvey.

Conclusion

To succeed in obtaining more appointments by telephone you must:

  know your prospects and their business;

  have a definite reason for asking for the interview;

  have a planned approach;

  have a main benefit to stress the need for the appointment;

  be prepared to listen, and don't pounce. (It might be that the prospect is about to give you an interview when you interrupt.)

  smile when you talk on the telephone;

  talk a little slower than usual;

  if not making headway, ask questions;

sound enthusiastic. Your enthusiasm will vibrate over the wires and will do more than anything else to get that appointment for you.

The obtaining of appointments is a challenge to all salesmen – a challenge which, if accepted, can lead to a far greater volume of business.

CHAPTER 6

Dial Human Relations

We can dial a telephone number and receive advice, news, weather reports, sporting results, recipes, and the latest stock market prices. If however, the GPO were to advertise *dial 1111 for improved human relations*, it would be taken out of service within a few months because of non-usage.

Why would it fail?

1. Because we all believe that we get along splendidly with everyone, and therefore we need no guidance on this subject.
2. We do not agree with the fundamentals of human relations, thinking that it may mean being hypocritical.
3. In this tough modern world there is no time for the niceties.
4. 'I believe people must take me as they find me.'

Let me make one thing clear: If all the books on Human Relations were placed end to end they might reach the one man or woman who carries out all their teachings.

As we are human beings with human frailties, all we can do is to strive for a better understanding of ourselves and other people. From this understanding stems the ability to *get along with people*.

There should be no necessity to press home the need for human relations in telephone selling, if it were not for the stands taken by so many people under the above 1–4 headings.

Does the ill-mannered hotel receptionist ever believe

that she is in the wrong? Of course not. It is those woeful, polite, subservient strangers in the queue, waiting to see if they can obtain accommodation, who are always discourteous and demanding. Does the snapping, tight-lipped shop assistant believe that she is rude? Of course not. She is a paragon of virtue in her own eyes, and if only other shop assistants she meets when she goes shopping were like her, all would be well in the retail world.

Robert Burns once wrote: *Oh wad some Pow'r the giftie gie us to see oursels as others see us.*

Every telephone salesman must be introspective enough and honest enough to be able to pinpoint his human relations weaknesses. A little difficult if he uses the excuse, 'Why should I change? It would be hypocritical of me to smarm all over people.'

Good human relations does not mean being weak or subservient. It only means acting towards others as we should like them to act towards us.

The salesman who says, 'They must take me as they find me' might discover that no one wants to take him anywhere.

No buyer would say to a telephone salesman:

'You sound belligerent;'

'You are argumentative;'

'You are impolite;'

'You are too familiar. . . .'

They have a far better way of showing their criticism, they put down the receiver, and don't buy.

It is true that in this modern tough business world there is no room for niceties if, by niceties, we mean unctuous flattery; but there is always time for courtesy, and usually it is those blunt, curt people who expect the most courtesy from us.

Why should anyone buy from us – agree to our requests for immediate payment of an account – accept our excuses for non-delivery of goods – if they feel antagonistic towards us?

Someone once said, the only man who can afford to forget human relations in marketing is the one with a monopoly – with traders beating at his door for supplies. But monopolies are few and far between these days, and they rarely last, anyway. Most salesmen have strong competition.

The way to beat the opposition is to have the best possible sales presentation, plus a likeable personality. Over the telephone a prospect only warms to us because he likes either our voice, our attitude, or the choice of words we use.

Good Telephone Manners

What do *good manners* conjure up in your mind? A heavily built, well fed Victorian gentleman saying to his wife, 'The gel will have to go, she doesn't know her place'? Or Lady Highmost writing to *The Times* to complain that young people these days don't stand to attention when she enters a room?

Divorce yourself from these thoughts. Having good manners does not mean being servile, and to be ill-mannered is not the prerogative of the young. Many people are not discourteous intentionally, but they lack awareness.

The telephone salesman must have that awareness, because good telephone manners win customers.

You're not sure? Don't you quickly reach boiling

point when someone treats you brusquely, stares through you, keeps mispronouncing your name, belittles you, or gives you curt attention? Of course you do!

You may now ask, 'What is this all about? This book is about telephone selling, not moral values.'

One goes with the other. If we are not conscious that we irritate and annoy people, how can we influence them to our way of thinking?

Let us take a few examples of bad manners, or lack of courtesy in telephone selling:

We can smoke or eat a biscuit while telephoning, and if you think this is unusual you haven't seen many the modern telephone salesmen at work, or you haven't listened to someone munching at the other end of the line.

When a salesman speaks with a cigarette dangling from his mouth he can strain the hearing of the prospect, trying to catch the muddled sounds hissing past half-closed lips. 'Sorry', says the salesman, who inhales deeply, splutters, and coughs. That would be all right if he were selling coughs.

It is bad manners to use endearing phrases to a telephone operator, thinking that they will win her over.

It is bad manners when somebody's name is mispronounced.

It is discourteous to ask a prospect to hold on while the telephone salesman searches for a price list.

In spite of what the cynics say, people do like good manners in others. And remember, *we* are *they* to our prospects and customers.

Politeness never yet lost the telephone salesman an order. Lack of this quality has caused many a telephone receiver to be slammed back on to the cradle.

It travels

A song which has been passed down through the ages has the words, *a smile will go a long, long way*.

The song writer wasn't thinking of a telephone call when he wrote those words, but amazing as it may seem, a smile does travel. The caller smiles, and the listener can *hear* it. Well, he doesn't actually hear it, but some extra sense which we all possess tells him that there is a friendly fellow on the line.

The telephone salesman must not only smile, but he must act as if he is selling face to face. Grimace, gesticulate, raise the eyebrows – these characteristics are personal, and they can almost be pictured by the listener from the tone of the caller's voice, because we alter the tone of our voice when we smile, or become annoyed.

Most people do smile often when they speak on the telephone. A mother, talking to her daughter, will automatically smile when told of what that little scamp of a grandson did this morning, and the daughter knows her mother is smiling.

You *can* communicate a smile. Byron wrote:

And o'er that cheek, and o'er that brow
So soft, so calm, yet eloquent
The smiles that win. . . .

Byron was not thinking of the telephone salesman, but for all that, smiles do help to win – orders.

Enthusiasm

We all know that there is nothing so contagious as enthusiasm – except the lack of it. If the telephone salesman cannot be enthusiastic about his product or service he should find another job. This applies particularly when he is trying to make an appointment. If you make your proposition sound a great opportunity for the prospect, he will see you. If he feels that you are just making another routine call he will not interrupt his routine to make an appointment with you.

The enthusiastic salesman not only smiles when selling, but his eyes light up because he is enjoying himself.

When Edison was developing the incandescent light he kept on experimenting and would not be side-tracked. After some thirty thousand experiments he had still not succeeded. One of his assistants lost his enthusiasm and said, 'Mr. Edison, why go on? We have made thirty thousand experiments and we are no nearer the results.'

'No nearer the results,' shouted Edison with great enthusiasm, 'we've had marvellous results. We now know thirty thousand things which won't work.'

The telephone salesman must always remember that he needs his enthusiasm most when the going is tough. Enthusiasm, more than anything else, can turn an average salesman into a super-salesman, because it is that enthusiasm which will urge him to improve his presentation, improve the quality of his voice, and master the techniques of telephone selling.

Tact

There is a Chinese proverb on tactlessness: *although there exist many thousand subjects for conversation there are persons who cannot meet a cripple without talking about his feet.*

Tactlessness in any walk of life is harmful. In telephone selling it is an order loser.

It is tactless to be too familiar.

It is tactless to use Christian names even when the buyer makes the first gesture, without his invitation to use his first name.

It is tactless to make remarks when selling such as: 'That sounds a bit Irish.'

'You must be a Scotsman, you drive a hard bargain.'

Jewish people are not won over when the telephone salesman uses Jewish expressions, and the Welshman doesn't want to be reminded that *Taffy was a Welshman*.

It is tactless to correct a word wrongly pronounced by the prospect, by giving the correct pronounciation immediately afterwards.

It is tactless to. . . .

There are a million of 'em, as Durante used to say. Don't you use any one of them.

Listen

Of all the self disciplines we need to succeed in selling, the discipline of listening more and talking less is one of the hardest to master.

The reason is obvious. We are always so interesting; we have such a fine story to tell; we always intrigue our listeners; we are so humorous; we had such a wonderful holiday; we had such a strange experience; AND, the other fellow is such a bore. It is so hard for us to understand that the other person feels just like we do.

When friends are battling for tongue time, the one who is least sensitive always wins. You have to be insensitive to other people's feelings to be able to pump word after word at them and not give them a break for a reply.

The salesman with the funny-man complex wants you to hear his stories, yet he always wants to cap yours before you reach the punch line. The articulate crusader – it doesn't matter what he or she is crusading for – will not give you time for his ideas to be answered. That's life.

Now we don't change our spots when we become telephone salesmen. The complexed funny-man, the insensitive crusader, will still want to monopolise the conversation.

While it doesn't matter much in everyday conversation – the worst thing that can happen is that our friends avoid us – in telephone selling if you are unable to be a good listener you can become just a good loser.

There is an old tag, *you don't have bad prospects, they have bad listeners*.

Never finish a prospect's sentence for him. Don't let your impatience show with 'yes, yes' interruptions, they are commands for him to speak more quickly. Never attempt to over talk the prospect; let him be solo, don't make it a duet.

Intent listening will help you to pick up the buying signals. Also, if he talks he is interested. When he stops talking he has replaced the receiver.

When the conversation is two-way, you know that he is involved in the sales presentation. You can listen yourself into appointments and sales. Listen most of all when you have asked a question. If you have talked through the answer you may have misunderstood what the prospect has said. You may continue selling when the sale is ready for closing.

I once asked a psychiatrist why people talk too much. I could not understand his reply, because he talked for twenty minutes without a break using psychological jargon which he understood, but I did not. When he had finished I said, 'That was all foreign to me. Can you sum it up in a couple of words?'

'That,' he answered, 'would be like asking a government department to simplify a law. There can be no simplification, but if you want a generalisation, then the person who talks too much does so from fear – fear of stopping and not being able to restart, fear of appearing inferior, fear of the interruption that he cannot handle.'

If it is true that we can only conquer fear by recognising it, then perhaps recognition might help the non-listener to talk less and to listen more.

You will recollect that in the chapter on *Voice Production* it was explained that by emphasising a word, by altering the sound of words, you could change meanings. This applies just as much to the prospect as to the salesman.

The prospect might say, 'Really, I don't want it,' which might sound half-hearted. It could also be a buying signal.

But if the prospect snapped *really*, and then emphasized *don't*, you might as well ring off.

By half listening, the first sound from the prospect could be mistaken for the second, and the salesman might then ring off when the order was just around the corner.

Listening can be called an art, but it is an art which can be acquired by all telephone salesmen. It only needs consideration – consideration first of what you are saying, and then equal consideration of what the prospect is saying, or asking. A good listener wins respect, achieves a friendly relationship with his customers, and learns the lesson that the easiest way to sell is to allow the prospect to *buy*.

Little Things Mean a Lot

It always delights us when meeting someone again after a period of time has elapsed and he says, 'I remember you very well, you had just started work for Smith & Sons and you were very happy. Also, I remember the day we met was your first wedding anniversary. . . .'

We almost shout with pleasure as we answer, 'What a fantastic memory.'

Most of us haven't got a good memory, so in business we have to rely on diaries, secretaries, note-pads, and even, sometimes, a string around the finger. The telephone salesman should always keep his records up to date. This applies not only to the orders he receives, but to repeat orders, special sales promotions, and any information relative to the buyer, the buyer's secretary, and other members of his staff. If, by chance, the buyer should say, 'I'm celebrating this evening, it's my birthday, but don't ask me how old I am . . .', make a note of it. A year later on that day you can wish him a happy birthday.

If his secretary is going on holiday, make a note. When she returns and you are speaking to her on the telephone, ask her how she enjoyed her trip abroad. . . . If the buyer has been away ill, show interest in his illness when he returns.

But it must be a sincere interest, not an on-and-off switch. It does no good to ask after his health and then, before he has finished detailing his sufferings, to interrupt with, 'The new carbons were really appreciated by the girls. . . .'

It is not time-wasting to make these enquiries of the buyer and his staff. It is only time-wasting when you talk about *your* holiday, or *your* illness. He is not interested in you, but you are interested in him for two reasons: The first, because it is good business; the second, because a habit, good or bad, can develop into being an integral part of a complicated human being. What sometimes begins as an act of salesmanship can become a part of our nature, and we are all better for being really interested in other people.

Human Relations

As mentioned earlier, thousands of books have been written on this subject, right down the ages. They have been written by social workers, teachers of religion, psychiatrists, psychologists, behavioural scientists, and lovers of humanity. Although they don't agree on all aspects of human relations, they mostly concur on one truism: *we like people to like us*. But the salesman doesn't have to sell his soul to be liked. All he has to do is to stop antagonising others, so that he won't be disliked.

Everyone can master the basic principles of human relations in telephone selling. They are so simple:

Be courteous
Smile when you talk
Be enthusiastic
Be tactful
Be a good listener
Be reliable
Remember little things

CHAPTER 7

Answering Objections

There is still a school of thought which advocates the old theory of welcoming objections as proof that the prospect is interested and is seeking further information. The prospect, according to this thinking, may even want to buy, and is using the objection as a challenge, to eliminate the possibility of making a mistake.

Modern opinion disagrees with this viewpoint. Unless a very weak objection is raised the prospect is making a point which the salesman must destroy. For example, the objection might be:

'I can buy cheaper elsewhere.'

The standard answer to this objection is to prove to the prospect that he doesn't only buy on price. There must be other factors such as quality, delivery, service, and confidence in the supplier. The price differential is narrowed and it is proved to the prospect that he should not consider the price of the product, which may be £50, against one that he can buy for £45. All he has to consider is the £5 difference, and the benefits he is getting for that £5. A good, sensible argument and one which will succeed time and time again, but the salesman is still implying that the prospect is naïve, doesn't understand his job, lacks business sense, and is indecisive, which sometimes can make a prospect dig his heels in and refuse to buy even when he knows that his objection is not valid. Therefore, never welcome objections, always try to forestall them. Provided the prospect only *thinks* the objection, no harm is done if he is proved wrong. It is when he *voices* it that he is likely to stand his ground. The telephone salesman should, therefore, build into his presentation answers to possible objections. This is the strength of the selling sentence technique. The elaboration of the step which will follow the sentence can so easily be changed.

If, for example, you know that your product has a feature which the prospect might consider to be a weakness, incorporate this weakness as a selling point. When you know that the prospect will raise an objection because of bad service received from your company in the past, bring it out into the open yourself. For example:

'Mr. Lee, as you know we have, in the past, had difficulties in meeting your delivery schedules. It is a problem which faces every company now and again, and it caused me a considerable amount of worry on your behalf. You will be delighted to know, Mr. Lee, that I can now assure you that you will receive supplies within three days of ordering.'

The salesman, having raised and overcome the objection, will continue immediately with his sales presentation. He must never pause to allow Mr. Lee to make any comment about bad deliveries. Best of all, he should switch to a question which in no way refers to the delivery problem.

'By the way, Mr. Lee, do you still find red is in demand?'

The salesman will now have achieved a dual object. He has forestalled the objection, and has taken the prospect's mind away from it by asking a question on another subject.

Here is another example:

'Mr. Jenkins, you have the reputation of being a very keen buyer, may I ask you a question?'

'Yes.'

'Do you buy *only* on price?'

No buyer will give an unqualified 'yes' to this. The answer will most probably be:

'No, I buy on value.'

The salesman can then continue:

'That's fine, Mr. Jenkins, because it is value I want to talk about.'

Some salesmen invite objections by breaking fundamental rules of telephone salesmanship. Here are the pitfalls to avoid:

Do not ask irrelevant questions

All too often a salesman will ask a question which invites a negative response. For example:

'Is the line selling well?'

Whether it is or not, the buyer, fearful of adding to his stocks, sees an easy way out and replies:

'No, I'm afraid it's sticking. Ring me again next week.'

Do not ask questions which can annoy the prospect

It is so easy to upset someone who is nôt keen to buy or to make an appointment. For example:

'Mr. Brown, you cater for the lower end of the trade, don't you?'

The salesman may well have slotted Mr. Brown's business in the right category, but Mr. Brown may like to mislead himself into believing that he also has a good class trade. He will, therefore, disagree with the salesman, and cut the conversation short.

Here is another example:

'Mr. Jones, you would like your office to be more productive, wouldn't you?'

Mr. Jones would, but he will rarely admit directly that there is room for improvement in his offices.

Be certain you can handle replies to questions

During research for this book I heard a telephone salesman saying:

'I'll call any time to suit, Mr. X. When may I come along?'

'Thursday, 8 a.m.'

Pause.

'I'm sorry, I'm afraid I can't manage that.'

Another example:

'You can have any colour you like, Mr. X.'

'I'll have black.'

'Oh, that's one we don't do now. There's no demand. . . .'

Answering Objections

In spite of your care in preparing your presentation, including asking the right questions, you will still get objections. Your planning is to minimise them. There are techniques for handling difficult objections.

They can only come under one of five headings:

Not interested

Can't afford it

Can buy better elsewhere

Dissatisfied with previous transaction

Delay excuses.

All objections are derived from these five main reasons for not buying.

'*Not interested*' can mean:

'Not interested in your product'

'Not interested in any similar product'

'Not interested because your price is too high'

'Not interested because you have a technically inferior product. . . .'

If the need is present and the objection is, '*Cannot afford it*,' it can mean that the prospect cannot afford to buy it from you, because:

He is temporarily short of cash

It is out of his price range

He would buy if it were cheaper

He could buy later. . . .

'*Can buy better elsewhere*' could mean:

Your quality is not good enough

Others have better designs

It does not meet with his specification.

Dissatisfaction with previous transactions might be a result of:

Difficulty in obtaining deliveries

Being unduly pressed for payment

Having had service problems. . . .

Delay excuses:

The prospect wants to consult his partner, director, a member of his family, experts, professional advisers, etc., etc.

The telephone salesman must evolve skills to answer these objections.

Hear it Out

Let the prospect voice his objection in full. In spite of the limitation of time you must not *pounce*, because of your eagerness to tell him that he is wrong. Let him expound on his objection, he may even sell himself off it. For example:

> 'I made up my mind not to deal with your people again. Your representative definitely misled me, and I couldn't even get an apology from your sales manager. I'm not blaming you, you've only just joined the company. . . .'

The prospect is giving the salesman an immediate opportunity to ease the customer back into a selling situation, firstly by ego building:

> 'Mr. James, it is very good of you to say that. You are obviously a fair-minded man, and I am sure, therefore, that you will see me for a few minutes to allow me to explain how things have changed, and how we can now be of better service to you. May I call . . .?'

Keep Quiet

There is something very dramatic about a pause, and something very disconcerting about silence over the telephone. If you wait for a few seconds before replying, there is always the possibility that the prospect will add to his objection and give you the hidden objection – the true reason for his not buying.

Repeat Objection

Be sure that you understand the objection. The prospect is not taught to obtain 'yes' responses. He can only assume that you and he are both on the same wavelength.

> 'There is no point in my seeing you, I'm full up with insurance. I'm getting on in age, and I've only got myself to think about.'

But the salesman doesn't listen carefully. He only hears the first few words, 'I'm full up with insurance' – a standard objection to which he immediately gives the standard reply

'I'm sure you will agree, Mr. Garth, that you would increase your insurance if I could show you how your policies could be rearranged. You might even save money. . . .'

But the main point raised by the prospect was, 'I have only myself to think about,' and that should have been the link on which the salesman should have based his reply.

'Mr. Garth, I appreciate that as a good businessman you are carrying a lot of insurance, and that you have only yourself to think about,' (pause here for any correction, then continue) 'I assume that you are a widower, Mr. Garth?'

'Yes.'

'Have you any children?'

'They're all grown up.'

'Grandchildren?'

'Yes.'

'Well that's fine then, Mr. Garth, because that is one of the things I want to talk to you about – how you can safeguard your future – and one doesn't know one's span of life, or how inflation will take its toll of income. Also, there is a special benefit that you can confer on your grandchildren without affecting your own income. May I call . . .?'

By repeating the objection he takes the sting out of it, but more important, he makes certain that he has understood it, and that he can, therefore, answer it completely.

The Apparent Agreement Technique

Whenever an objection is raised, tension creeps in. No buyer will admit it, but we all have a sense of caution that tenses us before we arrive at a decision. Therefore, the salesman must relax the buyer. The buyer raises the objection and expects an argument. The salesman also tenses as he senses the order veering away from him. To take the tension out of the objection the telephone salesman should use the 'apparent agreement' technique.

In a few words, he indicates that he is inclined to agree with the prospect. The prospect, scenting victory, relaxes.

The 'apparent agreement' technique is based on an elaboration of three words:

'I agree but. . . .'

Although the words may vary, the application is always the same:

'I quite appreciate the reason for your thinking that it would take up too much space, but. . . .'

'You are quite right, Mr. Thomas, in thinking that because the circulation is limited you would not get results, but. . . .'

'Mr. Smith, it is quite true that extra labour might be required, but. . . .'

The 'apparent agreement' technique takes the tension out of the objection.

The Boomerang Technique

The telephone salesman uses the prospect's objection to strengthen his case, turning the objection into a sales point. This is how it works:

'*I can buy cheaper and have a quicker turnover.*'

'But surely, Mr. Brown, that is the very reason why you should stock our products. You will make the same profit with half the effort, resulting in your assistants having more time to serve other people.'

'*Your delivery is too slow for me.*'

'Mr. Loveday, that is the very reason why you should buy from us. Our products are always in demand, and that is why we are slow in delivery. Also, they sell quickly. But by ordering well in advance you can be certain of supplies, and can keep ahead of competitors. It is for this reason that I am telephoning you now. . . .'

Praise the Prospect

When you link courtesy to ego-building the objection will not loom so large in the prospect's mind. Use these words:

'That is a very good point, Mr. Smith. . . .'

'I appreciate the very fair way. . . .'

'You are a very keen buyer, Mr. Jenkins, and I understand your objection to opening an account with a relatively small company, but. . . .'

'I know that a man in your position is always very busy, but I only need ten minutes to explain. . . .'

Ask Questions

You can turn an objection into a sales point by asking a question, or simply by saying, 'Why?'

'I'll speak to my partner about it.'

'Why, Mr. Brown?'

'I don't want any more insurance.'

'Why, Mr. Smith?'

'We're overstocked.'

'But you do like our products, Mr. Johnson?'

'Yes.'

'And you will stock them again when your stock levels are lower?'

'Of course.'

'Then your only concern is at placing an order now.'

'Yes.'

'That's fine. We can look ahead together and plan for future deliveries. May I call to see you . . . ?'

'I can't afford a new freezer.'

'I appreciate that, but you are interested in saving money, Mr. Loveday, aren't you? And if I could show you that a freezer could pay for itself over a period of time you would consider the proposition, wouldn't you? May I call . . . ?'

The professional salesman never welcomes objections, but by a complete analysis of his product or service he either forestalls the objection, or knows the technique to use as the occasion demands.

The following are extracts from calls made by telephone salesmen showing how they handle objections:

(a) Overcoming Difficult Situations

The fuel (petrol/diesel oil) commercial market is one that is dominated by delivery, service, and price considerations. Differences between suppliers are minimal. This situation applies to many other products or services.

In these circumstances a common objection to applications for initial interviews is *satisfaction with the existing supplier*.

A successful approach is often achieved by recognising the objection (by market knowledge, survey, and observation) before it is presented by the prospect.

'Mr. Harris, you demand and get a fast delivery service on your petrol and diesel requirements. It is for that very reason I would appreciate the opportunity of meeting you. This is Larry Williams of the Apex Oil Company.'

'You're right about delivery, but price also matters. I've got to get a good rebate.'

'Of course you have, Mr. Harris, and I know you get both these requirements from your existing suppliers.'

'I do. I've dealt with them for nearly ten years now, and I expect to go on buying from them for the next ten years.'

'Your loyalty is praiseworthy, Mr. Harris. Have you considered the situation should any one of a variety of reasons prevent your suppliers from delivering on time? Reasons possibly beyond their control – can you risk your business coming to a stop?'

'You've got a point there.'

'Look, Mr. Harris, let me come along to ensure that we have a record of your product requirements, delivery points, and current rebates. Then we can agree trading terms so that you can count on your needs being met should any emergency arise.'

'Yes, that's a good idea.'

'May I call on . . . ?'

(b) *Delay Excuses*

'Good morning Mr. Young, this is Harold Lester of the ABC Pneumatic Tool Company. I should very much like the opportunity of meeting you. May I call . . .?'

'What do you want to see me about?'

'Mr. Young, I want to show you how our company has been able to increase overall production by up to 30% for some twelve thousand eight hundred furniture manufacturers, not only in the U.K. but throughout the U.S.A. and Europe.'

'It sounds interesting, but we are so busy at this time of the year; to try out new ideas would only disrupt production and put us further behind with our deliveries. Come and see me in about three months.'

'Mr. Young, it would seem that you have a production problem right at this moment. If I can guarantee an immediate increase in productivity – and by immediate I mean within an hour as there is virtually no break in time with our tools – this would interest your company, wouldn't it, Mr. Young? May I call . . .?'

(c) *Not Interested*

'This, Mr. Prospect, I can well appreciate. But that is exactly what many of my clients said when first I spoke to them. You will appreciate that I cannot explain my proposition over the telephone, and it is for this reason that it would be in your interest for us to meet and see how you can benefit, as many others have already done. Now initially I don't require very much of your time. Would Thursday at 2.20 p.m. be suitable, or Friday morning at 10.20?'

(d) *Send Details in the Post*

'Yes, Mr. Williams, I will certainly send a brochure to you describing the general background of the company, and how we have helped many other people like yourself. This will enable you to acquire background information on our service, and when we meet I shall be able to show you exactly how we can help you specifically. Would Wednesday or Thursday . . .?'

'I am sure, Mr. Brown, that you are already receiving a great many brochures through the post and they can be most useful in detailing a proposition generally. I know you will agree, however, that our service is so personal to you and your own requirements that it is far better if I show you how we can help you. May I call . . .?'

The prospect will listen more readily to your presentation if he can save face and still maintain his authority.

He saves face when you forestall the objection, or when you use a technique which, instead of making him more stubborn, makes him ready to agree with you.

CHAPTER 8

Incoming Calls

A first impression means so much. Often, quite irrationally, we like or dislike a person on sight. Messages flash through the mind that:

she's putting on airs

he's acting a part

she looks bitchy to me

he's too dynamic for my liking. . . .

How ridiculous it is to come to such conclusions on such little evidence, and our judgement is so often proved wrong.

Have you ever taken an instant dislike to a fellow holiday maker, then one day you are thrown together and find that you have been mistaken, he isn't such a bad fellow after all. Generally, we are not given the opportunity to fathom the true man behind the façade. We go on our way, disliking him for ever.

Our attitude towards companies can be coloured just as quickly. When we telephone a store and are greeted curtly, told to hold on, neglected, we begin by being angry with the operator, and end by damning the 'whole bloody inefficient store'.

Every incoming telephone call is a sales opportunity – an opportunity to win goodwill, smooth down a dissatisfied customer, help build the morale of a salesman, or obtain an order. In every case a mind must be influenced, and that is what selling is about.

The telephone operator is given the first opportunity of creating the right impression. That can be difficult for her if she is sitting cramped in a dingy, draughty, reception office. For a girl to give of her best she should work in bright surroundings, be comfortably seated, and be left alone. All too often the telephone area is a meeting place for other members of the staff who want to gossip.

On joining a company the telephone operator should be given a booklet of helpful advice. This could include the following information:

(a) Always realise that you are one of the most important members of our staff, and that you can do a great deal to help our business to run smoothly.

(b) Calls for executives should be put through direct to the executive concerned unless special instructions have been given for them to be accepted by a secretary.

(c) The recipient of the call – departmental staff, secretary, or executive – will wish to greet the caller by name. If this is unknown, a request should be made in the following manner:

'May I tell Mr. Alert who is calling him, please?'

Never:

'Who is it?'

'What is your name?'

'Sorry, I can't put through without knowing your name.'

(d) Ask the caller to spell his or her name, if necessary. The correct information must be passed on to the ultimate recipient of the call.

(e) Please help us to give good service to callers, by not eating, smoking, or drinking while on duty. If you begin to eat a piece of cake or to suck a sweet, and the switchboard light gives a warning glow, you will either have to keep the caller waiting, take the remnants of the food or the sweet out of your mouth, or go on eating. It is far better not to begin the cycle.

(f) There will be occasions when the switchboard is very busy. You will feel harassed and, sometimes, irritated by the lack of courtesy of some of the callers, but please try very hard to keep calm at all times. It is better for the signal to keep flashing than for you to take a call which you cannot adequately service. The best way to keep calm is to smile. That will relax you.

(g) You are being supplied with a departmental chart and a list of names of those members of the staff most likely to receive telephone calls.

(h) Do not take messages. If you cannot contact the individual and there is no one else in the department, ask the caller for his telephone number and tell him that he will be called back as quickly as possible.

(i) Never screen a call. That is part of the duty of a secretary, when acting under instructions from her chief.

(j) It is most important that you service all calls. If a caller prefers to hold on instead of being called back, while you try to contact the executive concerned, advise that caller every thirty seconds that you are still trying to locate the executive. Never leave the caller wondering if he has been cut off or not. Also, he may wish to change his mind and ask to be 'phoned back.

(k) Always remember, there is no substitute for telephone charm.

These are basic instructions which can be adjusted to suit the policies of individual companies.

It Applies to Everyone

A book of helpful advice on telephone usage should also be given to members of the staff other than the telephone operator. It could be based on the points:

(a) Bad communication is the cause of many major and minor disputes and problems. Because the telephone is a means of communication, everyone should remember its advantages and disadvantages (both for incoming calls and inter-company calls.) One disadvantage is that while one executive may not visit another in his office, or make a journey to visit a supplier, he will hold lengthy conversations over the telephone, keeping the line engaged and, perhaps, stopping an important customer from contacting the department.

Telephone conversations should always be brief, but brevity does not mean curtness or rudeness. It is unusual to take notes of telephone conversation messages, therefore, instructions over the telephone must be clear and precise so that there is no subsequent misunderstanding.

(b) When the telephone bell rings in a department it must be answered immediately. Telephone operators become frustrated neurotics or bad-tempered savages if there is no co-operation from the office personnel and no one bothers to answer the call of the ringing bell. The staff type, chat, file, and check, and all because 'Betty isn't here to answer the telephone,' and 'Betty always takes the calls in our office.' If remonstrated with they excuse themselves:

'It isn't my job.'

'I don't know anything about it.'

'I'm busy.'

'I have an urgent job to do for Mr. Topper. . . .' and so on.

Members of the staff should be told that they are all responsible for servicing a telephone call. Everyone is involved in helping to make the company more profitable. Even if someone from another department is the only person available in an office, he or she should take command and pick up the receiver.

(c) When answering a call, give the name of the department followed by your own name.

'Service Department, this is John Smith.'

But that can sound curt, so always add:

'May I help you?'

Do that even if the caller is a colleague, because politeness is contagious.

(d) When you are advised by the telephone operator of the name of a caller, the greeting can be made more personal:

'Good morning Mr. Harvey, this is John Smith, Service Department. May I help you?'

(e) If satisfying a customer's needs requires the obtaining of information from files or associates, remember to service the call. Return to the telephone at frequent intervals to apologise for the delay. If, then, it becomes obvious that the enquiry cannot be dealt with in a reasonable time, suggest 'phoning back later with the information, and *always keep that promise.*

(f) When taking a call for a colleague, avoid saying: 'He'll call you back.' Settle the query yourself if at all possible.

(g) Always advise the telephone operator if you leave the building, and the time of your return.

(h) Never ask the telephone operator to take messages for you.

(i) Never leave a receiver open while you discuss a problem with other office personnel.

(j) Ignore colleagues who try to attract your attention or to interrupt you while you are in conversation with a caller.

Complaints

Every organisation receives complaints, some justified, some not, but all the people who complain are convinced that they are in the right. Sometimes they are rarin' to have a fight. What is ignored by many companies is that a complaint put right can be a customer retained. Why spend huge sums on advertising and strive for new business, perhaps to make up for losses caused by customers who are dissatisfied and have decided to buy elsewhere? And a customer will go elsewhere if he feels that he has a complaint which is not being dealt with fairly.

Don't greet the caller with:

'What is your complaint?'

'What is wrong?'

'What's the trouble?'

Do keep to the standard greeting:

'May I help you?'

Handling Complaints

1. Your company should give clear cut instructions as to what decisions you may make. A dynamic managing director will give fairly broad discretionary powers, otherwise called *delegation*. Without these powers a caller will be passed from one person to another, no one being willing to accept the responsibility of taking action. The instruction should be that everything possible must be done to satisfy the customer, and advice should only be sought if the decision you have made is not acceptable to the customer.

2. Listen carefully. Let the caller talk himself out. He may run out of steam, and then he will be more amenable to reason.

3. Never interrupt, however unfair the complaint may be. It is difficult to restrain yourself from saying:
   'That isn't right.'
   'But we did deliver.'
   'The parcel left here perfectly packed.'
   'It's the way you washed it.'
   Refrain from comment until you have heard the whole story. Jot down notes, if necessary.

4. Never lose your temper. It will not change the attitude of the caller, and can only result in a dissatisfied customer. It is sometimes difficult to remain calm and customers can often be unfair, but to be successful in business is always difficult.

5. Begin by believing that the customer could be right. This will help you to remain calm. Too many receivers of complaints believe that their company is always in the right.

6. Show interest in the complaint. Show sympathy as well, if necessary.

7. If you cannot give an instant decision explain what action you are taking.

'I am sorry, Mr. Brown, that this has happened. I will check with the accounts department and ring you back.'

'Mrs. Jones, from what you have told me there must be a fault in the product. There will be an immediate investigation, and I'll ring you back.'

8. Having promised action, you must take action. Do not put matters off while you deal with something else. Tackle the problem right away, or there is the risk of it being filed and the customer neglected. If you telephone back quickly, this alone will take some of the irritation out of the irate customer, even if you can only offer a compromise settlement.

9. If you are in the wrong, apologise quickly and unequivocally.

'I am sorry, Mr. Johnstone, we have really let you down, and there is no excuse. I cannot blame the computer or a strike, it was a human error. I can only apologise once more and assure you that we shall do our best to see that it will never happen again.'

10. If the customer is obviously in the wrong, then try to save his face.

'Tests have shown, Mr. Smith, that the material was burned, but if I were in your place I shouldn't believe that, I should be certain the material was faulty. I am sure you are a very fair-minded person, so may I send you a copy of the report?'

'I don't want a report — I want a new suit.'

'Mr. Smith, I am sure you will agree that there is no point in seeking expert advice if it is going to be ignored. I'll tell you what we'll do: If you like to send the suit to an independent research laboratory for a test we'll pay the fee if we are proved wrong. Is that reasonable?'

'Well – yes – I suppose so. . . .'

'Look Mr. Smith, let's settle the matter while we're on the telephone. We will repair it for you free of charge. That's fair, isn't it?'

The aim must always be with a complaint, to *settle it quickly to the satisfaction of the customer*.

The Secretary

Good secretaries are hard to find, and once found they should be treasured. The good secretary will be able to make decisions, know her boss's plans, thoroughly understand the business, and be able to handle people. There are, however, many shorthand typists who could be very good secretaries if their responsibilities were recognised and they received training instead of reprimands when things go wrong.

Most infuriating to executives is receiving wrong telephone messages, or the right messages with the wrong names.

All executives must keep their secretaries advised as to their comings and goings, and never fix appointments without telling their secretaries.

Without this information a secretary cannot deal effectively or honestly with incoming calls.

These words are taboo:

'He's at a conference.'

'I never know where he is. . . .'

'He was here a few minutes ago.'

'I think he'll be back by four. Who is that?'

No one ever believes the last statement, even if it is true. If possible, when callers cannot be connected with the chief, the secretary should tell the truth, because the truth *sounds* true:

'He's with the works manager at a meeting.'

'He's with a customer in the showroom.'

'He's just left for the factory.'

'He's with our Dutch agent.'

If a caller is holding on the line until an executive is free the secretary must, like the operator, service the call. She must indicate from time to time how long she thinks it will be before her chief is free.

A good secretary makes certain that her chief is the executive who can deal with the call. Often customers and suppliers telephone an executive because they know him personally, or because they want to speak to a top man with a query, when it can just as easily be dealt with by someone else.

The secretary must not say, 'What is it about?' but she can say:

'He's on the other line at the moment, Mr. Harris, (pause) is it to do with accounts? (sales query, delivery query, advertising query, etc.)'

Even if the secretary has made a wrong guess, the caller will nearly always correct her and explain the reason for his call. The secretary can then say, 'To save you holding on, Mr. Harris, I think it would be better for me to put you through to Mr. Parsons. He will be able to help you right away.'

A secretary will always remember that her courtesy

and efficiency on the telephone will reflect on her chief and also on the image of the company.

If she takes calls in a general office, the typists should be instructed to stop typing while she has the call transferred. It is bad communications when a caller is told, 'I'm sorry, I cannot hear you because of the typing.'

Make the caller feel welcome, even if you know that he is a miserable curmudgeon who is always complaining.

'Oh Mr. Clark, I'm so sorry, but Mr. Best is on holiday. May I help you?'

'Mr. Willis, I'm so sorry but Mr. Williams is at our Dunstable factory. Mr. Clifford is here, would you like to speak to him?'

Whenever possible a secretary should have the authority to fix an appointment without continually referring back to her chief. She should be in charge of his diary, and know his free time. This saves endless telephone calls and the alteration of arrangements.

A secretary must identify her department, name and position as soon as she picks up the receiver:

'This is Mr. Brown's secretary, Mrs. Lincoln speaking. May I help you?'

If a message has to be taken, remember the mnemonic:

who

what

when

which

Record *who* is the caller (name, address and telephone number).

Record *what* he wants (details of message).

Record *when* action was promised (return call, meeting, appointment, etc.).

Record *which* facts must be known by the chief before he can deal with the matter.

If a secretary has to transfer a call she must never say:

'Oh, you want Mr. Jones.'

or:

'You have the wrong person, I'll put you through to Mr. Jones.'

She will say:

'I'm sorry, you have the sales office. May I transfer you to Mr. Jones in the accounts department?'

Enquiries

Staff trained to handle telephone enquiries turn a high percentage into orders. Without training, this is liable to happen:

'Is that the sales office?'

'Yes.'

'I saw your advertisement for the new Denlon shirt, but I can't get any.'

'Where is your shop?'

'I haven't got a shop. . . .'

'I'm sorry, but we only supply through retail outlets.'

'I'm not asking you to supply me. I saw your advertisement yesterday. I went to three shops in the Victoria area, but none of them stocks your make. I'm telephoning to find out where I can get one.'

'Hold on.'

A pause. Someone else arrives on the telephone.

'May I help you?'

'I've just explained to the young lady that I want to

buy one of your shirts advertised yesterday – the Denlon. . . .'

'Selfridge's stock them.'

'But Selfridge's is in Oxford Street, and I'm in Victoria. Isn't there anyone nearer here?'

'Hold on.'

Three minutes later.

'Are you there?'

'Yes.'

'Bakers of William Street have them in stock.'

'But that's one of the shops I went to, and they haven't even heard of your shirt.'

'Well, I suggest you try Selfridge's. . . .'

If you can hardly credit this happening, telephone any manufacturer or distributor and make a sales enquiry. The odds are something like twenty to one that you won't get the right answer first time.

Although helpful advice should be given to the telephone operator and staff generally, to enable them to handle incoming calls, training must be given to all members of the staff likely to deal with enquiries. This applies equally to the junior recruit as to the most senior member of the sales office. All personnel must receive news daily, weekly, or monthly, of sales promotions. So often advertisements appear, or DMA shots are sent out, the salesmen are informed, but with the exception of a selected few, the sales office staff are left in the dark. That is the main reason for the caller hearing:

'Hold on. . . .'

'What did you say it was?'

'Where did you see it?'

'Are you sure you have the right company?'

There must be preparation. Available to all sales office staff should be brochures, advertisement cut outs, stock lists, colour charts, order packs, price lists, product changes. . . .

Enquiries are usually answered by a sales manager, assistant sales manager, sales office manager, or senior member of the office staff.

When someone enquires about a product or service, the telephone operator will transfer the call to the appropriate person. The snag arises when that person is not in his office. The call is then transferred to the general office, the telephone operator hoping that someone will be able to handle it. There must be that someone with all the facts available, so that the enquiry can be dealt with properly. If he, or she, is absent, then another person must take over. If properly trained in the technique of handling enquiries, any member of the staff should be able to deal with them in one of the following ways:

(a) Give all the facts required.

(b) Give facts, and arrange for a salesman to call.

(c) Ask for the telephone number so that the sales executive may call back.

    'Mr. Jones, I know Mr. Smith our sales manager would want to talk to you personally. May he call you back?'

The person accepting the enquiries will identify himself and, by the tone of his voice, show that he is interested and keen for the business. If this is left until all the information has been given, the caller may ring off hastily saying:

    'Thank you very much, that's all I want to know.'

Training must be given in product benefits, so that

members of the staff can close an order or make an appointment for a salesman to call.

This is how not to do it:

'I want a few details of your fire extinguishers. I'm afraid I'm not very technical, is it easy to operate?'

'Very easy. Mr. Sparks, may I send a salesman to demonstrate it to you?'

'Not for the time being. . . .'

That office clerk made no attempt to sell the product. He considered that he had fulfilled his task by telling the caller that the extinguisher was easy to operate, and by suggesting that a salesman should call.

But whenever an enquiry is made an extra benefit must be stressed. Let us deal with the enquiry again:

'I want a few details of your fire extinguishers. I'm afraid I'm not very technical, is it easy to operate?'

'First of all thank you for calling, Mr. Sparks. Your address is?'

'Main Stores, Clark Street, W.1.'

'Thank you, Mr. Sparks. By the way, do you employ female labour?'

'Yes, three girls.'

'Then you will be happy to know that our Model A extinguisher only weighs 4 lbs. It is as easy to handle as a small portable radio. Your smallest assistant could pick it up with one hand, easily. But picking it up isn't everything, Mr. Sparks, is it? You will want to know about the operation.'

'Yes, as I said, we're not very technical here.'

'It's as easy as opening a suitcase. You just flip a catch and press a button. It's as simple as that.'

'It sounds easy enough.'

'And what is more, Mr. Sparks, small as it is, it will put out an average fire in seconds – and after all, all large fires start with a small fire. I'm sure you will want protection right away, isn't that so, Mr. Sparks?'

'Well – er – yes. . . .'

'Good, then I suggest that I book an order for one – the price is £8 – and I'll arrange for an expert to call and advise you about siting it. He will also make sure that all your needs are covered. . . .'

An attempt must always be made to close an order on the telephone. The fact that someone has made the enquiry means that they are interested. By selling first and subsequently arranging an appointment the objection to a salesman is nearly always overcome. Even if an order cannot be booked over the telephone, the extra benefit of the service or product must still be stressed.

That Extra Service

In business today there is little to choose between many similar products or services. Whether you are in the office cleaning field or selling motor cars, insurance, or consumer goods, capital equipment or publishing, you are not so much ahead of your competitors that you can be certain of retaining any of your customers. You have some pluses and some minuses. So have your competitors.

The dynamic company will always get more than its share of the market because it will always look for that extra service – an extra service so rarely given by many companies, both large and small.

That extra service is to make sure that everyone who telephones your company is given a warm and friendly welcome, is dealt with efficiently and courteously, and is made to feel that the call is not an intrusion on someone's time, but a very welcome event.

'May I help you' must convey the message *I really do want to help you*.

CHAPTER 9

Outgoing Calls

'Mr. Johnstone, I have a call for you. I've tried to contact your secretary but she is not in her office.'

'Don't worry, Miss Hart. Who wants me?'

'A Mr. Arnold Coopersmith.'

'What does he want?'

Then, suddenly remembering his own rule that telephone operators must not waste time questioning callers, he adds hastily:

'Just put him through.'

'It's his secretary, I should think, Mr. Johnstone.'

'Doesn't matter, put her through.'

A pause, then a voice says:

'Is that Mr. Johnstone?'

'Yes.'

'Mr. William Johnstone?'

'Yes.'

'Will you hold on a minute please, I have Mr. Coopersmith for you.'

A minute passes, then:

'I'm sorry, Mr. Johnstone, but Mr. Coopersmith is out of his office. He was there when I made the call, and I'm sure he won't be more than a few seconds. . .'

Johnstone is about to replace the receiver when Mr. Coopersmith comes on the line.

'Mr. Johnstone?'

'Yes.'

'You don't know me, but our mutual friend George Clark told me to call you . . .'

Something like 20% of executives wanting to make

a telephone call ask their secretary or the operator to obtain the person they want to contact. This is *the* unpardonable telephone sin. Pomposity, thoughtlessness, a wish to show authority to junior staff – 'Get me so and so on the line' – a pretence of being too busy to dial a number, or lack of common courtesy – whatever the reason, this practice is a sure way of alienating customers and annoying friends.

A caller, whatever his position in an organisation, must get his own number, either by self-dialling or by asking the operator to give him a line. I am referring to calls to customers, although the rule also applies to telephoning many other people.

Sales Calls

Selling over the telephone other than making appointments can be divided into two main categories:

(a) *Repeat business*

Telephone salesmen regularly obtain repeat orders from stores, shops, hospitals, *etc.*, but except for special promotions, rarely initiate sales over the telephone. Selling to retailers, wholesalers, and direct to the public, is covered in Chapter 10 – *The Telephone Selling Organisation*.

(b) *Specialised Selling*

This entails closing deals over the telephone for which quotations may have been sent, or direct selling of services or products.

Specialised Selling, Prospecting

Telephone salesmen work from two lists, prospects, and past customers. The direct salesman, unlike the salesman of consumer goods and consumer durables, does not have the advantage of running accounts. He cannot telephone weekly for repeat business. If, for example, he sells an advertising sign to Bright & Company, it is doubtful whether he will be able to sell another sign to Bright & Company for several months, possibly years. The same would apply to blinds or canopies for shops. Replacements may only be needed every five years or more. Additional vending machines, additional fire extinguishers, additional intercommunicating units, cannot be sold on a regular repeat basis, but they can be sold over a period of time. However, the telephone salesman must still always remember to *use his users*. Past customers are better contacts to make than prospects. Customer cards must, therefore, always be kept up to date and keyed for extraction at the appropriate time. Before telephoning a customer the salesman will check the card, and then work out his hinge. It is sub-standard selling to telephone and say:

'You have had our canopy fixed for four years now . . .'

'I'm sure it is time for you to have another cigarette machine in your canteen.'

'Our Review of Industry is being published on 1 January. Last year you took a half page, would you like a full page now in the new issue?'

These approaches could be changed by thinking of a good hinge.

(a) *The Window Display Hinge*

'Mr. Barker, when I passed your shop on Tuesday I did admire your beautiful display of colourful ceramics. Do you change the display often?'

'Yes, we find it attracts attention.'

'Mr. Barker, because it is so successful you will want to enhance the colourful display by changing your canopy now to one of our new multi-coloured designs. It will line up with any display you make. This means that more passers-by will stop and admire . . .'

(b) *Exhibition Hinge*

'Mr. Smith, were you able to visit the Vending Machine Exhibition?'

'No, I couldn't manage it.'

'What a pity, I was looking forward to seeing you again and showing you our new unit with the armour plate glass front, which means that more cigarettes will be sold from it. It is the equivalent of a modern window display. You told me about your canteen extension, but I didn't want to let you have another unit until our new model was on the market. Delivery at the moment is slow, but I will . . .'

(c) *The Concession Hinge*

'Mr. Wilson, you will be pleased to know that the new Review of Industry out in January can help you in two ways: Firstly the circulation is being increased by 10%, but we have not increased our advertising rates; secondly, you can now have a full page facing the copy. This is a special concession to you, Mr. Wilson, as a regular advertiser . . .'

Plan, Plan, Plan,

There is no substitute for pre-call planning. It is the

only way to sell effectively. Get the facts, find the hinge, pinpoint the main benefit, and close quickly.

Cold Canvassing

Cold canvassing, whether by personal calling or telephoning, is never easy. The salesman having to call cold has to have an extra attribute – strength of character, determination, perseverance – call it what you will, but it means the toughness to accept many 'noes' to obtain just one 'yes'.

The telephone salesman with the wrong mental attitude curses his luck at being in a job in which so many calls are wasted. Soon, he is demoralised. The professional telephone salesman believes that every call is profitable, it is only a question of averaging out. He looks at it this way:

If an order is worth £20 and he has had to take nine 'noes' before getting a 'yes' on the tenth call, then every call has earned him £2. That is the right mental attitude.

Remember, I am now referring to selling direct on the telephone, not to obtaining appointments, which is much easier.

Planning for Cold Canvass Calls

First must come the perfection of a sales presentation, and then a further study of the market. What is the best time to telephone a prospect? This can vary from business to business, and it is not possible to lay down a hard and fast rule. Every telephone salesman must carry out his own market research. There is rarely a time, for example, when a housewife is completely free from duties if she has a large family, but it may be found that when she returns from her shopping and taking the children to school, about eleven o'clock in the morning might be the ideal time.

Only continual research on the part of a telephone salesman will help him to cut out time wasting calls. Some telephone salesmen will be able to work all day, while others may only be able to work for two hours in the morning and evening, depending on the type of prospect they are contacting.

The aim is to make as many calls as possible, that is why the rule for the telephone salesman is that after he hears six rings on the telephone and there is no reply he should cut off and try someone else. Time is so important to him.

It has been found by many telephone salesmen that store buyers may be contacted more easily between 4–5 p.m. than before 11 a.m. when they are seeing representatives, and they are usually in their departments or out buying during the early afternoon. Doctors, on the other hand, are best telephoned before they start their morning rounds or just after the evening surgery. Between 9–10 a.m. has been found to be a good time to contact top executives, while the owners of retail shops prefer to be called before 9.30 a.m. or early in the afternoon before the housewives return to shopping after lunch.

But no telephone salesman can work rigidly to a time-table. He must believe that his products or services are so excellent that the prospect will *want* to speak to him whenever he calls. By providing himself with a work pattern, however, he will be able to concentrate his efforts during those times when his calls will be best received.

Set Targets

When selling direct you must set yourself a daily target and never sell yourself short. There can be many excuses for replacing the receiver on the cradle.

'Not feeling too well.'

'Everyone's busy at this time of the year.'

'No one wants a 'phone call while there's a strike on.'

'It doesn't seem to be my lucky day.'

If every author who sets himself a daily target, as all authors do, stopped because he lacked inspiration or had a headache or he wanted to go for a stroll, few books would ever be written. The telephone salesman, like the author, creates, because a sales presentation is a creation, and hopes to close his story with a happy ending – an order.

Set yourself a target, and keep to it.

Leads

The life blood of the telephone salesman is leads. He will use classified telephone directories, business registers, trade journals, house magazines, newspaper advertisements, estate agents, chambers of commerce – he will also observe and note down new shops opening, change of occupancy, or a house decoration which is taking place, but his main objective is always to obtain leads.

The successful telephone salesman is a joiner. He will join clubs and trade organisations. He attends meetings and listens to lectures. He enjoys doing these things, but he also has the objective of obtaining leads.

'It's been nice meeting you, may I give you a ring sometime?'

'Do you mind if I ring him and mention your name?'

'Perhaps you know of someone interested in . . .'

'I'll let you have a copy, and then telephone you . . .'

Most people like to be helpful. If they are asked for advice they will readily give it. If asked for leads, they will try to help.

Last thing every evening the telephone salesman will prepare his work for the next day. He will not want to waste precious minutes during the morning selling time by *leaving things till to-morrow*. He will prepare a list of contacts for calls to be made. He will also check his presentation.

Are any changes to be made?

What will be the main benefit at each call?

What will he use as a hinge?

The hinge, to the telephone salesman selling direct, is just as important as it is to the salesman calling on his customers for repeat orders, or trying to obtain appointments by telephone.

With some prospects he may use the 'letter hinge', with others, the 'recommendation hinge' or the 'special offer hinge'.

The cold canvass salesman must keep to the rules:

(a) Careful preparation
(b) The right presentation
(c) The right hinge
(d) The right prospect list
(e) The right main benefit
(f) The right mental attitude.

SERVICING CUSTOMERS

It is less expensive to service existing customers over the telephone than by personal calling. The larger companies in the consumer field have their own telephone sales division. This aspect of telephone usage is covered in Chapter 10, *The Telephone Selling Organisation*, but companies in every market will find it well worth while to maintain good customer relations by better use of the telephone.

The formula is simple:

Use the buyer's name

Identify yourself

Give benefits of new products and new promotions

Thank buyer, and indicate when you will telephone again.

REVIVING INACTIVE ACCOUNTS

A buyer will never object to a telephone call expressing concern at not receiving his business. All inactive accounts should be telephoned.

'Good morning, Mr. Bristow, this is Alfred Thorpe of Cray Brothers. The manager of our order department has told me that we haven't had an order from you for three months. This concerns us deeply, and I am telephoning to find out the reason, Mr. Bristow . . .'

ADVANCE INFORMATION

A sales journey time might be six weeks, or a salesman may only make a visit three times a year. This leaves room for a competitor to take away business. A good way of keeping customers loyal is to use the telephone to advise them of new advertising programmes, TV features, new products, new designs, new technical factors . . .

'Mr. Leslie, I am telephoning you specially because I wanted you to know quickly about a new feature of our unit which will be on the market next month . . .'

'Mr. Wise, you will shortly be receiving full details of our dynamic new TV advertising campaign, which will bring you a lot of business. I wanted you to be one of the first to know our plans . . .'

REPLYING TO LETTERS

A shortage of skilled shorthand typists is often used as an excuse for the delay in replying to a letter. Some business firms think it sufficient if a brief, almost curt acknowledgement is sent. How much better to telephone, whenever possible. This action saves time, pleases customers, and can even cut costs.

When an enquiry is received through the post, many sales executives dictate letters which may be typed a day or so later. Precious days are lost before the prospect receives the information he is seeking. A telephone call could be much more effective in helping to capture an order while a competitor is still dictating his mail.

Letters of Complaint

Whenever letters of complaint are received it is important that they are dealt with quickly. Nothing eases a delicate situation more than for a customer to receive a telephone call offering him an apology or an explanation.

However well a letter is written in reply to a complaint there is always the possibility of it being misunderstood. Also, from the time the letter is written until a reply is received could be seven days. This could turn a simmering customer into a boiling-point customer.

Whenever possible, a letter of complaint should be dealt with immediately by the use of the telephone. The way to handle the complaint is as covered in Chapter 8, *Incoming Calls*, but the approach will be changed.

First there are some rules which must be adhered to:

1. Make sure the letter is fully understood.
2. Find out the facts of the case.
3. List all the points you wish to raise with the customer.
4. When making the call, restate the salient features of the letter.
5. Answer the complaint fully and effectively.
6. Make certain that the customer is satisfied with the explanations given, and the action to be taken.

You must now consider what your approach will be.

'Mr. Curtis, I have just received your letter and I must apologise right away for what has happened . . '

'Mr. Brown, I have just received your letter and if I were in your shoes I should be feeling just as you do . . .'

'Mr. Smith, I have only just received your letter and I cannot make any excuses for the lateness of our delivery to you. I can only offer you an explanation . . .'

'Mr. Jones, I have just received your letter and I am so sorry to hear of your complaint. I am sure that as a fair-minded man you will want to hear quickly our side of the story . . .'

Whether you are in the right or wrong, always begin

with an apology. Even if you are in the right there must have been some misunderstanding for the customer to write a letter of complaint.

COLLECTING ACCOUNTS

Every efficient company is tightening its credit control. An adequate cash flow is all important, and to maintain it every effort must be made to ensure that debtors settle their accounts as quickly as possible.

A collection policy might be that all accounts one month overdue will be threatened with legal proceedings. If the account is not settled within seven days following, court action is taken. This could bring in the cash, but it could also lose customers.

No marketing director would accept a policy of continually threatening action against good customers who could always place large orders elsewhere. These days a credit controller has to work closely with the marketing team, although the credit controller must have the final decision as to whether or not an account should be closed.

Most credit controllers would have less worries if they used the telephone more efficiently for debt collection.

Letters, however well written, do not influence the hard core of slow payers, and are thrown into the waste paper basket by those not afraid of legal threats. They do have some effect on the managing director who still likes to *pay on the nail* whenever possible.

The weakness of a letter is that it often is not personalised, although, of course, this need not be so. A letter, in consequence, might seem fair-minded and kindly to the writer, but may be read by the recipient as a curt, blunt, demand for payment.

With companies having thousands of accounts, or where accounts are computerised, letters and reminders will still have to be written, and only a selected few can be dealt with by telephone. But most credit controllers can use the telephone with great success. The majority of people pay up more readily when spoken to in an understanding manner over the 'phone.

But the accounts collector must remind himself constantly that:

1. Debt collecting by telephone can only succeed if staff is trained in telephone technique. It is better to write letters than to allow untrained personnel loose on the telephone.
2. The collector must talk to the person who can pass the account for payment. It is no use having messages passed on.
3. He must not be put off by elusive debtors. He must keep on telephoning. The debtor, unless he does not mind his whole staff knowing that he is being pressed for payment, will eventually speak on the telephone. If he is very troublesome, one of his assistants should be asked for his private telephone number. He or she may not provide it, but the debtor will get the message.
4. He must know exactly what he is going to say, and have all the relevant details in front of him before he dials the number.
5. He must set up a definite procedure. For example, telephone calls might be made twenty-one days after statements have been submitted. If these rules

are adhered to, debtors will accept the calls as part of a normal business procedure.

6. There must be a close to the sale – because it is a sale – the collector has to influence the mind of the debtor to take action against his wishes. The close would be a promise to pay in full, to pay something on account, to send a cheque by return, or to give a definite date when a cheque will be sent.

7. The collector's job is to collect the accounts *and* to keep the customer's goodwill.

Problems and Solutions

The control manager faces many problems. In the main these will fall into the following categories:

White & Co.	Good customers, policy is to take long credit.
Black & Co.	Good customers, temporarily short of cash.
Green & Co.	Living on knife-edge and paying those suppliers first who worry them the most.
Blue & Co.	Customer who refuses to settle accounts because of a grievance.
Red & Co.	Good customer, but sometimes bad payer. A stop has to be placed on the dispatch of goods to them.

1. *White & Co.*

The accountant of White & Co., is not influenced by threats. Threatening will bring about the closing of the account, unless White's buyer insists on having the products. But few buyers stand their ground when faced with a policy of obtaining long credit which may have been laid down by top management.

Their accountant will ignore standard letters and even pleading letters, but regular telephoning can change the situation dramatically. A friendly relationship must be developed with White's accountant, and his help sought rather than demands made.

The approach should be:

'We are both doing our job, and we should help each other.'

If the demands are reasonable they will be met. The aim must be to extract a promise from the accountant every time he is telephoned.

The *Whites* of the business world have the cash, but want to make use of yours. Don't let them do it. They are usually proud of their integrity and standing, and they expect others to be humbled by their size and reputation. They can always pay if they want to.

Telephoning *White & Co.* is not a job for a junior. The aim is to get on first-name terms with whoever is in authority at *White's* and can sign a cheque or sanction payment. If this rapport is built up, while others are sending out letters, begging, pleading, or even whining for their money, payment will be made to you.

2. *Black & Co.*

There is always a debtor pattern. Usually, *Black & Co.* pays up promptly and that is why it is disconcerting when they begin to take long credit. *Black & Co.*, unlike *White & Co.*, have never made it their policy to make use of suppliers' credit to help finance their business, but while they may have had a successful year last year, during the current year profits may have dropped. If a bad year's trading follows a successful year, the taxes from the good year are payable at a time when trading and cash flow may be at a low ebb. This could be one reason why *Black & Co.* are temporarily short of money. It could be that they have heavy capital commitments, or have made a large bad debt. The reason for their slow payment should be discovered if possible. A check at Companies House will give some indication of the position, but the accounts will not be up to date. If it is believed that *Black & Co.*, are only temporarily short of cash, then the credit controller, when telephoning, should use the *Question* technique:

'Mr. Black, I always look upon your company as one of the most regular payers of accounts. Is there any reason why you are now withholding payment?'

Mr. Black will probably tell the truth, and the credit controller should then make a reasonable proposal:

'Mr. Black, you don't want me telephoning you every month. If we give you X days extra credit will you meet our account promptly?'

If the *Mr. Blacks* of this world make a promise to keep to a new arrangement, they will keep to it.

3. *Green & Co.*

A credit controller will quickly place *Green & Co.*, in the right category and will, therefore, make a rule that they must be telephoned within seven days of receiving statements, although the account may not really be overdue.

It must be made plain to *Mr. Green* that extended credit cannot be given. A promise must be extracted from him, and that promise must be payment by return. If it is not received, another telephone call must be made – daily calls, if necessary. This is the only way to get *Green* to pay without taking legal action.

4. *Blue & Co*.

These are the customers to be handled with kid gloves. Before telephoning *Blue*, a careful check should be made to discover if there is any grievance. Many customers withhold payments, sometimes unfairly, because goods are unsatisfactory, service poor, or a salesman's promise has not been kept. And sometimes the grievance is not known.

If it is suspected, the credit controller should say:

'Mr. Blue, you are one of our most valued customers. There must be a reason for your withholding payment. Please tell me what it is so that I can immediately put matters right.'

If there is any correspondence in the file it will often be found that promises have been made by salesmen which have not been kept. A promise must be extracted from *Mr. Blue* to send a cheque off immediately on the understanding that the matter will be investigated and put right. Also, the salesman concerned must be made to call on him within twenty-four hours to offer his apologies.

5. *Red & Co*.

The salesman must not be instructed to take the matter up with *Red & Co.'s* buyer. This can only cause friction between the buyer and the salesman, resulting in loss of goodwill.

Red's accounts manager should be telephoned.

'Mr. Smith, obviously your buyer does not know of our credit arrangements, and he has placed another order with us while the previous account is overdue. If you will send a cheque off today I will release the goods immediately so that your buyer will not be short of stock. I am sure you would want that, wouldn't you, Mr. Smith?'

Save His Face

Telephoning, then, is an effective system of collecting accounts. It can be less expensive than the cost of writing letters, and it gets results.

The telephone accounts collector must remember:

1. To be tactful.
2. He must not discuss the debt with junior members of the debtor's staff.
3. He must use such sentences as:
   'We are all in the same boat these days.'
   'You are one of our best accounts.'
   'We are also telephoned for payment. It's a vicious circle, and we must all help each other.'
   'You have such a fine reputation for paying promptly.'
   'I know I can rely on you.'
4. He must keep his temper however rude or ill-tempered the debtor may be.

An efficient telephone collecting service can not only improve a cash flow and reduce bad debts, but it can also help to increase business.

CHAPTER 10

The Telephone Selling Organisation

There are four fields of activity in which large scale telephone selling (25–100 girls employed) can operate.

(a) Manufacturers and wholesalers in food distribution, selling to retailers and caterers.

(b) Newspapers selling classified advertisements and, to a lesser extent, magazines and trade journals selling advertising space or subscriptions.

(c) Retail stores receiving incoming calls from customers and selling direct to their customers.

(d) Telephone selling contractors retained by companies on a fee or a contract basis to carry out campaigns.

Within the next few years the use of telephone selling will multiply again and again, as dynamic managing directors realise its effectiveness as compared to the high cost of selling through salesmen.

Although, in this chapter, we study the telephone structure of two large organisations, its principles can easily be adapted to the setting up and functioning of a small division of only two or three telephone selling girls.

The Telephone Selling Controller

A typical structure of marketing management is shown overleaf.

Although the marketing director is ultimately responsible for the successful launching of his company's products or services, it is the sales manager who will augment the sales on a day to day basis. Regional

Marketing Director

Export sales manager	Office sales manager	Home sales manager
	Regional sales managers	Telephone sales controller
	Salesmen	Telephone sales girls

managers under his control will supervise their areas, but the telephone sales controller will control all of the teams selling by telephone throughout the country. She will appoint supervisors and engage, train and motivate staff. Out of the eight companies whose telephone operators were examined only one had a man in charge of the team. It would seem, therefore, that the telephone sales controller will nearly always be a woman, whose skills seem more appropriate to the job.

Profile of a Telephone Sales Controller
The Telephone Sales Controllers I met when researching for this book had many characteristics in common. Before commencing telephone selling their backgrounds were:
(a) property negotiator
(b) assistant in a department store
(c) cosmetic representative
(d) telephone receptionist
(e) store demonstrator of electrical appliances

(f) secretary

(g) ladies' wear representative

One common factor was experience in selling or dealing with the public before becoming telephone sales girls and subsequently achieving promotion. It would seem from this evidence that although many highly efficient telephone sales girls have no sales background, this experience is advantageous if promotion is to be achieved.

The other common factors were:

(a) dedication to work. Three of them are married, the others single. They are prepared to talk telephone selling all of the working day, but the married girls claim that they drop the subject on returning home in the evenings.

(b) They are bright, very feminine, and attractive. The latter is obviously not essential for the ideal profile for a controller, but these career girls obviously set a fine example to their staff in dress and appearance.

(c) They are all articulate.

(d) They know how to get along with people.

When seeking a telephone controller, therefore, one should not on this evidence look for a tough hardbitten business woman, but rather, an articulate, attractive girl within whom runs a streak of human kindness and understanding.

It is not possible to build a successful telephone sales division without having a highly competent person in control, fully backed by her chief.

The Sales Team

All companies use similar procedures for engaging

staff. A few years ago advertisements for telephone selling staff were strictly formal.

EXCELLENT OPPORTUNITY FOR GIRL TO
JOIN TELEPHONE SELLING TEAM

or, just simply:

TELEPHONE SALES GIRLS REQUIRED

This has changed. Executives have caught up with the idea that advertisements must be attractive to applicants. They must have YOU appeal, and list many benefits.

Here is one:

JOIN A HAPPY TEAM

Our telephone sales girls have the opportunity of earning well above average incomes, winning prizes (a trip abroad is not unusual), building a really worthwhile career, and being happy in their work . . .

Here is a gimmicky advertisement:

TELESELL FOR BELLE

You may not be Belle, but your name doesn't matter. If you like using the telephone, if you have a pleasant voice, if you like working with a happy band of girls (and, of course, some men) you should call us right away. You might be just the Belle for us, which will mean for you, a good salary . . .

Here is a team-appeal advertisement:

JOIN US

Joan was once a secretary, Jean a model, and Carol an hotel receptionist. Joan, Jean and Carol are now highly successful telephone sales girls. Not only do they achieve a high reward for their efforts, but their work is stimulating, challenging and interesting. If you would like to join us . . .

A challenge advertisement:

YOU?

Have you a sparkling personality, the determination to earn the highest possible salary? You have? Good! If you have an attractive voice and like working with a happy band of telephone sales girls . . .

Although approximately 90% of telephone sales girls are found through advertisements, the balance of 10% are recommended to join an organisation by friends employed by the company. If the average is below 10% the controller should take a close look into the conditions under which staff work, and discover if they are really happy in their telephone selling.

But even with the near ideal telephone sales organisation turnover of staff is still heavy, for the usual reasons. Some girls are only seeking temporary work before going abroad or on holiday, others have babies, or a husband has to move to a new area because of his work. Because of this, a telephone controller should try to build up a reserve list of girls. Advertising means delays, and if there is a waiting list, vacancies can be filled much more quickly.

Most controllers agree on the profile of the girl most likely to succeed in the job.

Sociable.   Has other interests and a wide circle of friends.

Courteous.   It is easy to tell whether a girl is
                    courteous, when she telephones for
                    the vacancy, or at a meeting.
Endurance.   It can be wearying, selling over the
                    telephone hour after hour.

The background of the applicant, how many jobs
she has already held, family, will all give some indication of her endurance potential.

The clarity of her voice can be tested over the telephone, her temperament discovered by questioning.
A temperamental girl will never succeed in telephone
selling.

The following case studies will show how the
objective of finding the right girl and training and
controlling her are put into practice.

SMEDLEY ROSS FOODS LTD.

This company markets a wide range of canned and
frozen foods through wholesale and retail channels
and direct to caterers.

The telephone selling girl's work is mainly concerned with frozen foods. A few of the well-known
products of this company are fish fingers, beefburgers,
crinkle cut chips, and cod steaks.

The controller of the telephone selling operation is
Rosemary McColl. The following is a summary of one
of our meetings:

'Miss McColl, what is your title?'
'National Telephone Sales Supervisor.'
'And what are your responsibilities?'
'Briefly, the engaging, training, and motivating of
telephone sales girls.'

'You cover the whole of the country, which must mean that you travel a great deal.'

'Nearly all the time. I have to cover fifty depots.'

'The depots being, in the main, warehouses from which the stock is delivered?'

'Yes, and each one has its own telephone sales team.'

'Would you like to tell me how the team is made up?'

'The average number of girls for a telephone selling area is six, including a supervisor. Each girl works closely with a salesman in the field.'

'Do they sell only to retailers?'

'No, usually three girls and three salesmen sell to retailers and the same number sell to caterers.'

'How are the girls paid?'

'Salary, plus a weekly bonus. But there are other incentives. We hold regular competitions in which both the salesmen and their telephone selling partners take part. Prizes have included clothes, watches, even a continental holiday.'

'Obviously, by offering joint prizes you get a team spirit, and you also obviate friction which might occur if one girl got a prize and the salesman didn't, as they are both concentrating on the same customers. But there must be friction, surely?'

Rosemary shook her head. She answered:

'No, they really do work in harmony, with the aim of giving a good service to our customers.'

'The accent in the consumer field is, of course, on service?'

'Definitely. If we sell persuasively it is because we know that the retailer will leave himself short if we don't, when necessary, ask him to increase his order.'

'What do you mean by selling persuasively?'

'We may have a special promotion and a retailer may usually take a dozen of a product, but a girl will say, "I will send you two dozen." She doesn't ask what he wants because she knows what he can sell. That is why the liaison between the girl and the salesman is so important. He, of course, knows retailers' stocks and potential sales often better than they do themselves.'

'Tell me how the girls work so closely with the salesmen without having orders duplicated, or girls telephoning just after the salesman has left.'

'It's all very simple. The salesman visits his depot once a week, but he telephones his selling partner at least three times a day for a joint check. You see the salesman will only call on a retailer approximately every three weeks, depending on the retailer's turnover, but the telephone sales girl will call the retailer once a week, or in the case of a supermarket, twice a week.'

'How does the administration work?'

'There are two sets of customer cards. The salesman has one, and the telephone girl the other. Each morning the cards of the customers to be telephoned that day are given to the girls. The salesman, when he telephones, will be told which customers are being contacted. When he 'phones again later in the day the girl will tell him of the orders taken, so that he can up-date his cards. His is really a shuttle card, because he also returns his cards to the office regularly to be checked against the master cards. The result is that the retailers get good service and quick deliveries, and they are rarely out of stock. It is much less expensive to telephone for repeat orders than for a salesman to attempt to make contact weekly. That would mean, perhaps, doubling or trebling the sales force.'

'Do the girls find that the retailer is sometimes too busy to speak to them when they call?'

'No, he knows the time of day of each call and is prepared for it. Very quickly a friendly relationship is established between our girls and the retailers. The customers nearly always use the girls' first names.'

'How many calls do the girls make each day?'

'Between sixty and seventy.'

'How are the girls kept up to date about your regular promotions?'

'We have monthly promotions, and these are explained to both the girls and the salesmen at a meeting attended by the advertising manager and the regional manager. The meetings are held in a local hotel at about four-thirty in the afternoon. Also, news letters are sent out regularly, coupled with an up-dated presentation guide.'

'You have about three hundred lines in your range. How do you sell them to caterers?'

'They are divided under twelve headings, and the girls present a case usually dealing with one product under each heading. They could not possibly sell the whole range, but when they know that there is a special need for a product they persuade the caterer to agree to an appointment for one of our cookery experts to call.'

'How do you obtain your girls?'

'Mostly by local advertising, but we are very selective. I find I have to interview about fifteen girls to engage one.'

'What training do you give them?'

'We hold a week's course. We begin by providing company knowledge, then spend two days on product knowledge and invoicing procedures. The rest of the time is divided into dealing with objections, co-operating with salesmen, a question session, and sales presentation.'

'You do provide them with a sales presentation, then?'

'For special promotions we give guide lines, but we do explain that every call must use the standard formula

Approach
Interest
Product
Close.'

'Do demonstrations take place, or cameos?'

'Oh yes, we have many two-way telephone conversations, with a training supervisor or myself acting as a customer, either retailer or caterer. Sometimes we make calls to the girls, and other times they originate the calls to us.'

'Do your girls both originate calls, then, and accept in-coming calls?'

'Yes. I know that in some organisations each is a special function for different teams, but we find that it is quite easy for our supervisors to organise and to allocate incoming calls to the girls who are free at any particular moment.'

'Finally, do you have standard approaches?'

'Yes, for example, we never say to a retailer, "I am calling to find out what you need", but, "I am calling you for your tomorrow's delivery." '

Smedley Ross Foods Ltd., have a highly efficient telephone selling operation controlled by a highly efficient national training sales supervisor.

THE EVENING STANDARD

This London newspaper's classified advertisement department is claimed to be the *most modern and rapidly expanding one in Western Europe*, with the *most intensive training in the country*.

Judging from what I saw of their Telephone selling Division and the results which this division has achieved, they are certainly most efficient, and the department seethes with activity.

The controller is Yvonne Bolland, who has the title of Group Tele/Ad Manager. Seated in her office she explained with great enthusiasm how her girls had helped to build the advertising pages of the *Evening Standard*.

I asked her what criteria she set when engaging staff. She answered:

'When an applicant telephones she has to sound a nice person to get an interview. We work as a team here, and however good an applicant might be, I want to be certain that she will fit in well with the other girls.'

'But you are concerned with her background?'

'Not really. We employ an ex-model, an ex-actress, an ex-secretary – in fact, ex-almost everything. If a girl is an enthusiast and has a good speaking voice we can train her to succeed.'

'What training do you give?'

'The initial training period lasts a week, but there is continual refresher training.'

'Can you give me some idea of the induction training course?'

'I like to build morale from the beginning, so first we tell them why they have been specially chosen for the job, why they have succeeded where others have failed and, of course, we have to tell them about us – the newspaper industry generally, and classified advertising in particular – and the way we work. We explain the overall market and, of course, cover administration. Next comes one of the most important sessions, *How to Write Advertising Copy*.'

'You manage to do all that in a week?' I asked.

'Yes,' she answered, 'there is no mystique about copy writing, only common sense. It isn't difficult, it is quite simple to change an advertisement which is uninteresting into one which sparkles. We want our advertisers to use copy which gives results, and therefore, if their copy is not good enough we have to help them. We instil in our girls pride in their job, and their main objective is to help advertisers to achieve results, so that they give us more business.'

'Do you teach the girls a sales sequence during the induction course?'

'Most definitely. They have to keep to standard guidelines. Following the *Sequence*, we teach them

How to Answer Objections, and then we have demonstrations, with myself and one of the supervisors
acting the part of the advertisers.'

'You mention that you deal with objections.'

'Yes.'

'I should like to ask you how your girls deal with
one particular objection. You teach them how to
increase an order for a single insertion into a series
of four, on the understanding that the advertiser can
cancel any of the remaining advertisements after the
initial one has appeared if he or she has obtained
satisfactory results. Also, you offer a fifth insertion
free of charge if the results from the first four have
not been good enough. Am I right?'

'Yes.'

'Firstly, why do you make this offer?'

'To help the advertiser. If only one insertion is taken
and it is not able to bring results – and no one-off
advertisement can be guaranteed to bring in the
required replies – then the advertiser is dissatisfied
with the newspaper and he has also wasted a considerable amount of time and money. By offering the
additional advertisements with a cancellation clause
– and we accept the cancellation without question –
the advertiser will almost certainly obtain the
results he wants.'

'Fair enough. So now for my objection: I have
accepted your offer of a series, but I shan't have the
replies to the first insertion and be able to evaluate
them before the others appear. If I use a box
number there is an even greater delay, so whatever
happens it looks as though I am going to be stuck
with the four advertisements. Surely it would be

better for me to put them in one at a time with a period in between?'

'I don't agree, Mr. Tack. What are you advertising for – or pretending to advertise for?'

'We'll say a shorthand typist.'

'And you want the best available.'

'Of course.'

'And as a good business man you will want to see a number of applicants so that you can make certain of selecting the right girl for the job.'

'Yes.'

'And you want to fill the vacancy quickly.'

'Yes.'

'Then, Mr. Tack, that is the very reason why you should take a series, so that you will be certain of obtaining a sufficient number of replies from which which you can select your short list.'

I laughed, and said:

'I'm sold.'

'We also teach the girls,' said Yvonne, 'that if it is necessary they should suggest having two or three days between the first and second advertisements, so that the objection you raised is overcome.'

'They are taught copy writing, a sales sequence, and how to answer objections. What else?'

'We like them to suggest ideas for the layout of an advertisement – for example, semi-display when necessary. A good headline can also attract attention.'

'May I hear some of your girls at work now?'

'Of course.'

I was taken then on a conducted tour of the department, and listened to several of the girls selling.

There are three console switchboards, each controlled by a supervisor. The switchboards are modern in design and automatically search for a free line, so that the caller is kept on the line no longer than necessary and the girls, therefore, are continually occupied in selling. There are nine girls in each team. Some handle incoming calls only, others cold canvass for advertisements. There is also a girl to take the orders for cancellations, or changes in advertisements.

I asked Yvonne how the girls canvassing for orders obtained their prospect lists.

'Each morning they are given cuttings from the previous day's newspapers or magazines, and these provide good leads. We also give them prospect cards which list the names of previous advertisers, such as car showrooms, restaurants, cinemas, *etc.*'

'How do they approach someone who has advertised in another newspaper?'

'Firstly, they never ask if the advertiser is satisfied with results. Our girls are taught the subsidiary question technique. Listen now to Joan . . .'

I listened to a sale being made by Telegirl Joan (I have changed the name of the girl and the customer).

'Mr. Johnson, it's Joan Sims of the *Evening Standard* Classified Advertisement Department. You advertised your car in yesterday's . . .'

'Yes.'

'Is it a blue car, Mr. Johnson?'

'No, red.'

'Has it a radio fitted?'

'Yes, quite a good one.'

'How about tyres, are they in good condition?'

'Excellent condition.'

'Has it disc brakes?'

'Yes.'

The questioning went on for only a few seconds, and Mr. Johnson was obviously deeply interested, because Joan was talking about *his* car and *his* interests.

Quickly, she tied up the deal by suggesting an entirely different wording to the advertisement he had used before – one which highlighted all the car's main features.

Mr. Johnson said, 'I think it's worth twenty pounds more for all that, what do you think?'

'I think you're right.' And the order was clinched.

Next I heard a good sale to a car dealer who had not advertised for a week or two in the paper. His reason was:

'I'm short of stock, so why should I advertise?'

'That sounds reasonable, Mr. Smith. I suggest you advertise for second-hand cars to give you some cars to sell.'

Mr. Smith laughed.

'It isn't as bad as all that.'

'Have you a red . . . in stock, Mr. Smith?'

'No, only a metallic blue . . .'

It was the questioning technique again, and finally Mr. Smith agreed not only to advertise the blue car, but also one or two others that he suddenly found he had in stock.

The message from Yvonne Bolland was loud and clear: The success of a telephone selling department stems from the work of the telephone controller, who must be backed by a dynamic chief. When she, in turn, handpicks a good team, inspires and enthuses them, then they must succeed.

The overall need, however, is for the controller to be someone who is dedicated to the work of the division.

It is easy to find advisers who will assist with the type of equipment needed for a division, or planners who can plan the lay-out, but without someone in charge who can maintain the enthusiasm of the girls by continual training and inspiration, the equipment and the planning can never be used to best effect.

CHAPTER 11

Buyers Can be Difficult

Sometimes buyers are predictable, at others, unpredictable. The nervous buyer will always be nervous, the chatty buyer will always want to waste time talking about everything except placing an order. Their attitudes, therefore, to the telephone salesman, are understood from the moment the approach is made. But the unpredictable may change in temper or attitude as readily as a chameleon changes colour – kindly one moment, bad tempered the next. One chance remark can bring about this change. A seemingly polite person can become four-letter rude if he feels that he is being talked down to, or that a complaint he is making is being minimised. At times, therefore, all buyers are easy to sell to, and at other times they can prove to be most difficult.

We cannot change people, but what we can do is to recognise their strengths and weaknesses, their emotions and temperaments, so that we can help them to come to a decision in our favour. Success in all forms of salesmanship depends on our ability to motivate people. We can best do this when we can communicate with them in such a way that we can allay their fears, soothe their tempers, or feed their egos. In other words, when we know how to handle them.

The Logical Buyer

The logical buyer is a man with a clear, analytical mind, sometimes with a degree to prove it. But to the professional telephone salesman, no proof is needed. His incise questioning quickly categorises him.

With this buyer a salesman must be ultra-careful of the claims and statements he makes. No salesman should exaggerate, although many do, perhaps unwittingly. For example:

'It is noiseless, Mr. Smith.'

The logical buyer immediately answers:

'If it were noiseless it wouldn't work at all. There must be some sound from it.'

That sort of retort can set a salesman right back in his chair.

Here is another example:

'That means, Mr. Smith, that the interest rate works out at 14%, and it is tax free . . .'

'Can you guarantee that? It is only correct under present legislation. Are you able to assure me that there will be no change in the Law within the next ten years?'

And bang goes the sale on an investment plan.

The logical buyer must be sold to logically, and there should be no attempt to appeal to his emotions. Any claim which cannot be justified must not be made. A statement must not be so embellished as to give him the opportunity to criticise a minor point of your claim. For example:

'Everyone believes it,'

'It is a well-known fact in the trade . . .'

'It applies particularly to you in your profession . . .'

These remarks enable the logical buyer to interrupt with:

'Why do you say in my profession? Doesn't it apply just as much to men and women in all walks of life?'

Neither should you deal in approximations. Try to be exact. He will want to know exact costings, correct measurements, delivery dates which are not guesswork.

Although he will demand the fullest details, remember *you must not give them to him over the telephone*. The fact that he wants more evidence is an ideal opening for you. It is the reason why you want an appointment to see him.

With Mr. Logical, cut out all the padding. Give him information which is logical enough for him to give you an appointment.

The Semi-Tycoon

Most people think of the tycoon as the dynamic head of a self-built empire, but generally the people we meet when we sell are only half or two-thirds of the way up the ladder of success. Yet they like to act the part of the big chief, which is why they are called semi-tycoons.

They are often difficult to contact on the telephone and treat the telephone salesman as if he were one of their junior staff. If you request an appointment he will fob you off on to one of his assistants, just to show how important he is.

Standard ego-building techniques don't work well with him, although they may with his chief. With a semi-tycoon you use the *maybe you are not so great technique*.

At the approach, for example, you could say:

'Mr. Johnson, I am not quite certain whether you handle computer time or whether I should speak to Sir Sidney (his chief) about it . . .'

If it is suggested to the semi-tycoon that he has not

the power to buy when he is the buyer, he will indulge in self ego-building. He will not want the salesman to approach his chief and will make it clear that he is the man who makes the decisions. The salesman must then be ready with a subsidiary question to stimulate the semi-tycoon's thinking and arouse his interest. The rules are:

Allow him to build himself up to his chief's level.

Ask questions to stimulate his thinking.

Do not waste his time by asking questions which serve no purpose.

Let him believe that he is controlling the conversation.

The Complaining Buyer

The attacking complainer is the man who, as soon as you speak to him says:

'You're just the person I want to speak to. That last delivery of yours was so badly packed that the contents arrived damaged. They were unsaleable.'

'Give you an interview? I told your sales manager six months ago that I wouldn't do any more business with you.'

'The ad. didn't pull at all. I certainly wouldn't repeat it in your paper.'

We are not now dealing with a buyer who has a genuine complaint. We covered the problems of handling such a person in Chapters 8 and 9 on incoming and outgoing calls. The complaining buyer uses his complaint as a defensive weapon. He does not specifically pick you out for a fight. He uses the technique with every salesman he doesn't want to see or to give an order.

It makes him immediate master of the situation, and he finds it easier to turn down the request of the salesman for an interview or for an order.

Once you have classified the complainer, and have made the appropriate notes in your diary, you can always be ready for him.

It is of little use explaining to such a man that the goods were packed perfectly or that because he wanted credit for goods he couldn't sell, *he* was in the wrong, not the manager.

There is one effective way of handling this man. Let him first complain, and don't interrupt. Apologise, although that won't help, but it is courteous, then offer him something special:

'It is because we have let you down that I am telephoning you. I want to put things right. This is what I will do specially for you . . .'

The next time you call don't give him the opportunity to complain but say to him immediately:

'Mr. Smith, I am sure you had no further reason to complain of . . . I am looking after your requirements personally . . .'

Whatever you do you must not build up the complaint, but neither must you ignore it. Take either of these steps and he is ready to move in to get rid of you. The rule, then, is to *apologise briefly and then sell very hard on the special service you are offering him.*

There are only two occasions in selling when a customer's words are almost brushed side. One is when he raises a frivolous objection, and the other when both of you know that it is his standard practice to attack by complaining.

The Buying Bully

Bully Buyers are few in number. They must not be compared with the sarcastic buyer, or the rude buyer.

The bully buyer delights in squashing a salesman. He has his own coterie of suppliers who fawn upon him or have a friendly relationship with him outside business. He gives the appearance of hail-fellow-well-met, he is usually a good mixer both in pubs and clubs. At home he only shouts loud enough for his wife not to hear him.

He is a man who often tries to be boss at home, but rarely succeeds, and psychologists might conclude that this is one of the reasons why he likes bullying salesmen. But like all bullies, he is a coward at heart, and has to be handled firmly. It is no use kow-towing to him. If you have to do that it is far better to ring off and try someone else, because you will never win.

You must be prepared for his offensive manner, and sometimes, his swearing; always his abruptness. He will also want to do all the talking and will bait you about the quality of your goods and the prices you charge.

This man is not difficult to handle. You must not contradict him – not until you are well in with him, anyway – because that is just what he is waiting for to allow him to explode.

Keep on plugging away at your benefits. The more he shouts, the more you talk benefits, and never sound apologetic. Use such sentences as:

'You are a man who can make up his mind quickly, this is well-known in the trade, and this special line is just what you are looking for. You will also want quick delivery . . .'

'You will forgive me for saying this, Mr. Johnson, you are known as a tough buyer, but you are also known as a very fair-minded man, so you will allow me to explain . . .'

'What the hell do you want?' His opening greeting.

'We both want the same thing, Mr. Smith – extra cash, extra security, extra savings. All I want is five minutes of your time. If, after five minutes have passed, you don't want me to stay I'll go. Is that fair?'

The Indecisive Buyer

Most of us complain from time to time about the lack of attention given to us by shop assistants. They have a case, however, for sometimes feeling that they would like to karate-chop down a customer – the indecisive customer who will take up this and that, show an interest in one colour and then another, be certain that Y is exactly what they want, and then remind themselves that K might be more suitable . . . It is not that they are timid or frightened to buy, it is just that they are indecisive.

You will talk to many buyers like this on the telephone. They will call you to place an order and then be beset by a hundred doubts, while you have other customers waiting on the line. You will make a superb presentation and feel certain that the order is yours, and then he will hum and ha and if and but . . .

The salesman will always have to make the final decision for the indecisive buyer, who otherwise will be continually evasive, and able to make use of a whole list of excuses to help him.

'I'll talk to my wife.'

'I'll talk to my partner.'

'I'll consult my solicitor.'

'I'll definitely have it later on . . .'

When the indecisive buyer shows a preference the salesman must make his mind up for him, and forget all the other articles in the range.

When the secretary hesitates to make an appointment for her chief the salesman must make the decision for her.

'I appreciate, Mrs. Jones, that you are not certain of Mr. Wilkins' movements at the moment, but I'll risk that. Make it three o'clock – you did think he might be free then – and if I call and he can't see me, that's my bad luck.'

'You like the small size better – I'll send you a gross.'

'You won't have any worry, Mr. Brown, our actuaries have worked it all out for you and you know the high reputation of my company. You only have to tell us the amount that you can afford. £20,000 too high? Right, let's make it £18,000 . . .'

With the indecisive buyer you must act as his best adviser. Never let him down, and you have a customer for life.

The Talkative Buyer

If the telephone salesman is not allowed to give his presentation how can he close the order or get an interview?

To prevent a salesman from completing his sales sequence one type of buyer keeps talking. The sale is bogged down. The salesman believing in human relations may have asked the prospect if he enjoyed his holiday; the prospect will talk about his holiday for so long that there is little time left for selling. There is only time for the prospect to say:

'Call me next month.'

This type of prospect or customer will side-track the salesman in all sorts of ways, and the salesman cannot stem the flow of words. While a salesman must not be a pouncer and interrupt a buyer, there is a vast difference between pouncing and allowing a buyer to take control.

With Mr. Talker a salesman interrupts the prospect without offending him. He must wait until the talker says something that can be linked to a sales point. He might be explaining how the weather has affected his business. The salesman interrupts:

'Excuse me, Mr. Brown, I know you will agree that it is when the weather is bad and your customers stay at home that you have to do something to bring them into the shop. This is where I can help you . . .'

The talker may be interminably describing some technicality of his manufacturing process. He is bogging the salesman down in technical details. The salesman interrupts:

'It is obvious why you are technically so far ahead of your competitors. I can help you to beat them on price. May I call . . .'

The talker will only quieten down when he appreciates the strength of the salesman and his proposal.

The Too-Friendly Buyer

A buyer may be abrupt, curt, almost rude, yet he may still listen to a salesman's proposition; but the too-friendly buyer can make life very hard for the telephone salesman. He agrees with everything in a facile way.

His pleasant manner is a disguise. He knows it is hard for a salesman to tie him down while he is being so friendly. The timid salesman is always impressed with friendliness, and is easily put off.

It takes a strong salesman to overcome the too-friendly buyer; his strength will enable him to put his foot down and start to sell. If the customer agrees with him, he will ask for the order. When he doesn't agree, he will sell even more strongly.

The salesman knows this buyer for what he is worth and will not be side-tracked by his friendliness. Even at the risk of antagonising him, the strong salesman will carry on with his sequence.

You must win the friendship of a buyer, but the best proof of his friendship is when he gives you orders.

The Timid Buyer

The timid buyer cannot make a decision easily, and takes avoiding action. He should not really be a buyer at all. The more timid the buyer, the more decisive the salesman must be. Do not give him alternatives, his mind must be made up for him. He must be given a single course of action, and induced to take it.

The timid buyer's greatest anxiety is that he will make a mistake. This is understandable in a very small business where a mistake might cause considerable financial embarrassment, but store buyers, too, can be timid. They are scared of the merchandising manager's displeasure if they purchase the wrong stock. They are frightened of overstocking. They are afraid of opening new accounts.

Time must be spent on building Mr. Timid's confidence – confidence in the salesman and in his products.

This must be accompanied by tremendous enthusiasm. Some of this will, eventually, rub off on Mr. Timid, who will then summon up the courage to place an order on the telephone, or to make an appointment.

Talk to Mr. Timid of larger quantities than you hope to sell; he may be frightened at first, but when you then suggest a smaller quantity he will be relieved, and more inclined to buy.

The Silent Buyer

While the talker won't stop talking, his opposite number won't say anything. When the salesman explains the main benefit, the only answer he gets is a grunt.

You must make this kind of prospect agree with you. He must be brought into the sale. Even the most vociferous salesman cannot overcome the silent buyer and will eventually dry up.

The way to succeed is to sell by using a series of questions. Practically every sentence must be a question. At first the answer may be a grunt, but eventually the prospect must say something. He might be able to grunt a half-dozen times, but on the seventh occasion, tough as he is, the prospect must answer.

Ask questions, and soon the silent buyer will begin to talk. When he starts talking you know you are making progress.

The Bluffer

The bluffer is similar to Mr. Timid at heart. He deceives salesmen. He talks in large quantities, stresses that he buys in thousands, but he always delays making a decision.

Mr. Bluffer says:

'I don't believe in playing about. When I buy I buy. It's not worth my while opening an account with you for just a few gross. In six months' time I should be ready to give you a good order. Telephone me then . . .'

This is bluff. You must tie him down. He may want to place a small order but, having taken his stand, cannot easily reduce the quantity. Say to him,

'Mr. Johnson, I appreciate that you want to buy two hundred dozen, but if you will take my advice, don't. Two hundred dozen would not worry you, but it would worry me. One of my biggest accounts began in quite a small way. The buyer is a man like you, who knows his own mind, but I asked him to test out the market and find out for himself just how many he could sell in the course of six weeks. If you would begin with fifty dozen . . .'

The chances are that you will get your small order, but if you think it is wiser to wait a month or two to obtain the big contract, you will be sadly disillusioned.

You must tie the bluffer down to a small quantity initially, even if it goes against the grain. The big business will come later after his confidence in your products has been proved right.

The Stubborn Buyer

When the stubborn buyer has made up his mind, nothing seems to budge him. Any hint of criticism will lose the order. He would rather make a wrong decision than change his mind. His problem is psychological. He is afraid of appearing weak. If he has raised an objection he doesn't want you to prove him wrong. He is the kind of man who will tell you that he believes in admitting when he is wrong. Unfortunately, he always believes that he is right. The strength of your sales presentation enables you to sell to him. A presentation that forestalls objections lets him feel he is making all the decisions, all the time.

To know yourself, and to know your buyer, are excellent twin objectives for all salesmen.

CHAPTER 12

The Professional Salesman

Whenever the telephone bell rings in shop, office, factory, store, or warehouse, there is a sales opportunity; an opportunity to create goodwill, to close a sale, to handle an enquiry effectively, or to smooth down an irate customer. When anyone picks up the telephone to ring a customer or prospect, the same opportunities arise.

In the same way as British salesmanship has improved so much over the years, so will the standard of service given to customers by those who use the telephone get better and better.

Twenty-five years ago British salesmen were untrained and were being criticised continually, but now, the majority are truly professional. There are no longer derogatory remarks made about the men who spearhead our export drive. In this country the standard of salesmanship is, today, as high and sometimes higher than it is anywhere in the world. As our courses are held in thirty-four overseas countries we are able accurately to assess the standards of selling in these countries.

The modern British salesman has a high IQ, is ambitious, and works hard. He is also keen to improve his general knowledge of business. He not only attends courses on salesmanship, but in ever-increasing numbers is sent to courses covering such subjects as inventory management, credit control, accountancy, management by objectives, public speaking, letter writing . . .

AND TELEPHONE SELLING.

And that is what this book is all about . . .

Index

The
TACK ORGANISATION

is the largest training organisation of its kind in the world. It has twelve thousand client companies in the United Kingdom including many leading names in industry and commerce. Companies in the TACK group market products and services through every type of outlet and provide the up-to-date practical experience on which all training is based.

This practically, together with highly professional teaching methods, has largely accounted for the success and growth of the Training Division, which offers these courses:

■ FINANCE
Finance for the Senior Executive
Introduction to Finance for Managers
Cash Collection and Credit Control
Introduction to International Commerce

■ MANAGEMENT AND SUPERVISORY
Leadership in Senior Management
The Multi-Discipline Manager
Executive Development
Communication and Negotiation Skills for Managers
Motivational Leadership
Effective Supervision
Effective Supervision – Part 2
Effective Office Management
Effective Office Management – Part 2
Profitable Time Management
Executive Decision Making
Recruitment Interviewing and Selection
Performance Appraisal

■ COMMUNICATION
Effective Speaking
Effective Report Writing
Better Letter Writing
Better Use of the Telephone

■ SALES
Sales Training
Sales Training – Part 2
Selling to Industry
Selling to Industry – Part 2
Professional Sales Development
Profitable Negotiating
Professional Telephone Selling
Dealing with Customers by Telephone
Successful Territory Management
Selling to Wholesalers and Retailers
Selling Financial Services
Better Selling through Financial Awareness

■ MARKETING AND SALES MANAGEMENT
Field Sales Management
Field Sales Management - Part 2
Profitable Sales Management
Introduction to Marketing

■ SPECIALIST TRAINING
Caring for the Customer
Customer Relations for Service Engineers
The Executive Secretary
Introduction to Microcomputers
Training the Trainer

In-Company Training is provided in all these areas, specially designed to suit specific client requirements.

Open Courses are run regularly on most of the above topics, with mixed attendance by client companies from all areas of industry and commerce.

THE TACK ORGANISATION
LONGMOORE STREET LONDON SW1V 1JJ

Telephone 01-834-5001

A Full List of Cedar Books

While every effort is made to keep prices low, it is sometimes necessary to increase prices at short notice. Mandarin Paperbacks reserves the right to show new retail prices on covers which may differ from those previously advertised in the text or elsewhere.

The prices shown below were correct at the time of going to press.

All these books are available at your bookshop or newsagent, or can be ordered direct from the publisher. Just tick the titles you want and fill in the form below.

Mandarin Paperbacks, Cash Sales Department, PO Box 11, Falmouth, Cornwall TR10 9EN.

Please send cheque or postal order, no currency, for purchase price quoted and allow the following for postage and packing:

UK   80p for the first book, 20p for each additional book ordered to a maximum charge of £2.00.

BFPO   80p for the first book, 20p for each additional book.

Overseas   £1.50 for the first book, £1.00 for the second and 30p for each additional book
including Eire thereafter.

NAME (Block letters) ....

ADDRESS ....

....

....